G000151276

UNSUCCESSFULLY
SUCCESSFUL

UNSUCCESSFULLY SUCCESSFUL

Lessons from a never-enough
workaholic, corporate exec,
single mother's journey to
a life of balance

DONNA STAR

NEW DEGREE PRESS

COPYRIGHT © 2023 DONNA STAR
All rights reserved.

UNSUCCESSFULLY SUCCESSFUL

Lessons from a never-enough workaholic, corporate exec, single mother's journey to a life of joy and balance.

ISBN   979-8-88926-922-9 *Paperback*

            979-8-88926-965-6 *Ebook*

This book is dedicated to my beautiful children,
Hannah and Jordan, who gave me my favorite
job title of all time, mom.
I love you both endlessly.
And, to my dad, who loved me without
conditions or distractions, thank you
for bringing me into this world.

CONTENTS

INTRODUCTION

I quit my job after I met with an alternative medicine healer.

Well, it was probably a year later, but this appointment started the process. My son's comments and the concerned look in his eyes were really the final straws.

He said, "Mom, this is not normal. You need to leave your job."

This comment moved me to write my resignation the same day.

At the time, I was working on a project to help lead the integration of a company we had purchased into our company. It was, hands down, the least favorite job I have ever had. I liked the people and some parts of the work, but it was not a good fit for my skill set. It was the company's attempt to try and keep me in the fold, but I was miserable.

I didn't even know this type of doctor existed. My personal trainer, whom I have worked with for over seven years and knows me and my body quite well, suggested I try something different. I was game for trying anything because I was so out of whack that I was having trouble digesting food.

This was a doctor's appointment unlike any other. Joanie asked me a lot of questions and performed what I can only describe as a body scan. After what seemed like quite a while, she finished the examination. Here is what I remember the most.

She said, "the polarity in your body is way off."

I guess I already knew this because I could not eat my everyday staples such as salad. But what I didn't realize was this was my body's attempt to tell me to stop the insanity in my life. My body was telling me to stand up and listen to what I already knew in my heart and soul.

Corporate life was no longer working for me, and it hadn't been for a very long time.

Before the integration job, I led sales, ran regions of the company, and oversaw accounts and teams. A running joke was that I had held almost every position in the company. As much as I loved my clients and colleagues, I had a complicated relationship with my corporate life. I was never really fulfilled.

I had given my notice many times. I had to review how many times I left and/or had given my notice. The number was five! I left the company twice, but I ultimately returned because this place was like home to me. The three times I gave my notice, but did not leave, the company found other opportunities for me. I know how lucky I was to have a company support me and find ways to use my skills, but the last time I left in 2019 was final. My daughter was about to graduate from college, and I wanted to travel with her. My significant financial commitments to my kids were coming to an end, relatively speaking of course. It was time to go create the life I wanted after over thirty years of corporate life, although I had no idea what this looked like.

On a recommendation from someone new in my life, I investigated the iPEC coaching program. Truthfully, I signed up for the program because I had no idea what I wanted to do next. Signing up for this program would provide good air cover in conversations to show that I had something else in the works. I was used to having a plan. I was used to being busy. Quiet felt like purgatory because I was so unused to having time and space to do anything I wanted. I was a woman without a country. My busyness drove my sense of worth.

I took a leap of faith.

On day one of this eight-month program, I fell utterly in love. Coaching is the most aligned I have ever felt in my life. Helping people live their best lives is an honor and a dream. One thing I didn't anticipate was that training to become a coach meant I had to be coached. This makes so much sense because we are all works in progress, and I experience many of the same feelings and situations as my clients. I wasn't anticipating this, but it has helped to change my life in so many ways, which I will touch on in this book.

I have helped hundreds of people get more clarity about what they want from life and work. Life and work are connected, so I am specific in that I am not only a career coach. I am a coach who helps my clients create the life they want: to live more intentionally, to not let life run them but to take more charge of their choices and the way they show up in the world. I work with my clients to help them develop more confidence to find new jobs, end and find new relationships, get promoted, leave their jobs, and, most importantly, find themselves.

Coaching is the perfect blend of my experience because I have been in my clients' shoes—difficult bosses, promotions, demotions, recessions, turnover, office politics, hiring, firing, and all the stuff in between. Understanding and helping people was my favorite part of corporate life. And, in this process, I have found myself and my voice.

When I look back on my career, I feel tired just thinking about it. Being tired and busy all the time was a badge of honor for many corporate denizens like myself—back-to-back meetings, flights, clients, internal issues, you name it. If you aren't busy, you must not be valuable or be doing corporate right.

If you aren't crawling to the weekend as if to a tall glass of water in the desert, then you dialed it in for the week. That is what coaching does for others; it shows them the BS stories we tell ourselves to keep us exactly where we are. You don't have to work later than all your team members to show your undying commitment to the company. Suppose you leave early or even on time to spend more time with your family. In that case, you are modeling excellent behavior, allowing others to create the same dynamic for their own lives. The work will be there the next day and the day after. In your performance review, did your manager focus on the hours you worked or the results you drove?

Being happy outside of work increases productivity and overall satisfaction.

Coaching allows us to dismantle the stories that run our lives and provides the opportunity to look at things in a new light. Once you look at things differently, you become more aware and hopefully make better decisions. I want to shine a light on the work we can do to help ourselves and help us weather any inclement weather that comes our way.

Coaching empowers us to believe we are good enough already.

We deserve more just because we are, and we don't have to seek constant outside validation. If we shore up our insides and become our own best friend, can you imagine how wonderful this will feel? I can. I spent far too much time believing that beating myself up was the only way to move forward and be successful.

This book is for you if you are currently working in corporate and want to improve your quality of life. This book is especially for you if you are trying to navigate the political roller coaster of corporate life while trying to raise a family and live a more balanced life. Lastly, this book may be for you if you have/had parents or partners you consider workaholics. You will hear how my work/life affected my kids and relationships. You are not alone. I will go out on a very thin limb to say we take ourselves way too seriously. We spend an excessive amount of time keeping our voices in and ourselves small.

I was tired of keeping the real me hidden, and I certainly don't want that for you.

Once I finished the coaching program, I hired two coaches for myself. First, I started with a business coach, Jeffrey St. Laurent, who helped me set up the infrastructure of my business. One of the first things he had me do was start writing emails and creating an email list. He wanted me to write three times a week, but that was too much for my corporate group, who were already sinking into a sea of emails. I found that I liked to write, and people liked what I had to say, so with some encouragement, I decided to write this book. I have written every two to three weeks for the past four years. My list and following have grown. And I am happy to say that writing has become much easier and more natural for me.

My second coach, Tracy Litt, was also life-changing for me. She dug in and excavated all the BS programming I had incorporated into my body; you can't get too high because you know what comes up must come down. She helped me connect to myself in so many new ways that, at first, my system freaked out. I initially rejected this new way of thinking, but she stuck with me. Slowly, I changed my mindset, and became much gentler with myself, allowing me to grow exponentially. Working yourself to the bone was, in fact, not the only way to get ahead. No matter what anyone says, change is possible, but it is hard work.

I write about my life and career path as a single, workaholic mother raising two exceptional children while traversing and climbing the corporate ladder. I coach both men and women at every stage of their careers. I interviewed clients, friends, family members, former colleagues, and my children for this book. My children were a later edition to this roster. They had a front row seat to the crazy. Maybe I added them later because I was not ready to hear what they had to say.

We make life/work/relationships much harder than they have to be. In one of my favorite chapters, I talk about intuition more deeply. We all have access to intuition. Yes, we do. Intuition is when you can feel someone is angry or the hair on your neck or arms stands up. Knowing without proof that something is true is intuition. We all get signs of some sort. My "number" or sign is thirty-three, which often shows up in my life. Signs are all around us and within us. Let's stop ignoring them.

While you read this book, I hope you will learn valuable lessons along the way as I share my stories, research, and interviews. You are not alone in this world. You can make the changes you seek. I want to show you how.

We only have one life. Let's live it on our terms.

CHAPTER 1

THE BACKWARD/EARLY YEARS

Everything starts in our upbringing, right? I worked for over thirty years in corporate America. But my relationship with things and people began long before my work life.

The Tipping Point

I gave my notice for the last time in April 2019. It was the perfect storm for me; my daughter was graduating from college—no more tuition payments! My son was living on his own in Los Angeles. My job working on integrations was a horrible fit for me, and the company had recently sold, so I had a little extra money in my pocket. Combining all this with my body giving out, I knew it was the right time to make a move. The body always knows what is going on, if we would only listen.

I no longer wanted to prove to myself or anyone else that I was good enough. I was tired of being tired. I was scared. I was energized. I was ready.

It was my time.

Coaching is the perfect culmination of my training and my experience. Coach training helped me unlock all the years of bottled-up emotion—trying to be strong and show confidence and competence. On the first day of training, I crumbled into a heap. I allowed myself to break down. You would have thought I had it all—a great job, title, status, and all the silly trappings of that—but it never felt right because I didn't believe in myself. Part of my learning journey was to take a simple survey, the VIA Survey (Via Inventory of Strengths, 2004), which identifies your top character strengths based on positive psychology. I highly recommend checking it out!

The VIA Survey is the only free, scientific survey of character strengths in the world. Take this simple, fifteen-minute character test and discover your strengths here: www.via-character.org. Research shows that knowing and using your character strengths can help you:

- increase happiness and well-being
- find meaning and purpose
- boost relationships
- manage stress and health
- accomplish goals

My top character strength is humor, which is something that had been achingly missing in my life. And then, it hit me over the head—my why. Coaching is not just a career but my life's purpose. I want to help people *not* do the things I did. I want to help people realize we all have choices, even when we believe we don't.

I want you to say what you want to say and remember to live your life with some humor and levity. Enjoy your life now, not when something happens, not if something happens, but now—today. We are only on this earth once.

Maybe humor isn't *your* thing, but taking yourself too seriously likely is. And, my goal is to help change that for you because you deserve it.

Let me back up and start at the beginning. We all bring our childhood experiences into our lives. How did mine affect how I show up in the world today?

Let's dive in.

Where it all began

I am the youngest of three children born to two loving parents, but like every family, we had our stuff. It makes us who we are. I am the only girl, so I was adored right from the start by both of my parents and brothers—most of the time. My dad finally had his baby girl, and my mother had a kindred spirit in the house of all males.

Good start.

We lived in a peaceful neighborhood in a nice suburb outside of Boston. My mom was a bookkeeper, and my dad had his own painting business, which he had taken over from his dad. My oldest brother was labeled a genius, and my parents moved to our town with the best school system in the area, which may give you a hint of how important education was in my family.

Though my parents loved each other, they probably had no business being married. I highly doubt marriage counseling was a consideration at that time. My mother came from the original definition of a broken family and lived in a private school for kids who needed to live away from home because her mother was ill, and her father was absent. The youngest of four siblings, her parents separated early on in her life. Her father settled down with another family, and her mother died of cancer at a very young age. My mother never really disclosed too much about her childhood, but there were whisperings of physical and sexual abuse. My mother's sister, Kay, was rumored to be a "lady of the night" before she became a mother and then a swami. In our family folklore, Kay was questioned about this line of work. Her response was:

"Hey, we have to eat, don't we?"

My mother's siblings were not very close, and we did not see or hear from them often.

My dad was seemingly the opposite. He was the youngest of six in a loud, boisterous, successful, large Jewish family. Of course, looks can be deceiving. My father did not come out unscathed from his childhood either. I have heard stories of his mother making bathtub gin during Prohibition, my grandfather being abusive, both leaving their children for months at a time to head south for the winter and not leaving any money behind, and many, many other hard to fathom today, stories. My parents came to their relationship with trauma to spare. Both of them had mad tempers and unrealistic expectations of relationships and marriage, which is probably not the ideal environment to create a family.

My father was dedicated to my mother until the end, caring for her every need. During a rare hurricane warning, my dad drove several towns over to buy the only food my mother could digest in her final days. Her stomach was full of tumors. He didn't give it a second thought. He cooked, cleaned, did laundry, and anything else that needed to be done around the house. Despite coming from a very patriarchal family, he showed me it was possible to dismantle gender roles and still be a "man." By the end of my mom's life, all the noise and drama in their relationship had evaporated and all that remained was love.

There was a lot of love in my house, but it was also very volatile. The passion that must have brought them together was also infused with financial hardship and disappointment. Add in three active children and a long-term illness that would ultimately take my mother's life at the age of forty-eight.

We all have events that stay in our psyche. The ones I remember are that I had a strong need to be seen and heard. This was driven by being the youngest and only girl in a male-dominated house. We ate dinner together every night. One night in particular, I raised my hand when I wanted to talk. We were and are a rambunctious bunch. Heaven help the people who sit near us in a restaurant.

In elementary school, I developed a rash that needed medical attention. I had drawn the rash on with a red crayon. I don't remember my age when the next event happened, but I could not have been more than five or six when I ate a whole jar of orange-flavored St. Joseph's baby aspirin. It took me a long while to eat anything orange tasting again. What would these events have caused the parents of today to do? Was this a mental health issue that needed attention? These were not questions that parents or families asked about in those days.

I grew up in a neighborhood of active kids living on safe streets playing all sorts of childhood games, fluidly moving from one basement or house to another. One family had an above-ground pool, and another had a pool table and walls we could write on, so we were well set up for daily fun. We had many outdoor trails behind us that we used for sledding, with an accident thrown in here and there. All this was done without any parental supervision. We never locked our front doors, and despite the diminutive size of my family house, we were generally the hang-out house. We knew dinner was ready when we heard our names being yelled to come inside to eat. Who needed a cell phone when you had a mother with powerful lungs?

When we were older, our friends knew this was the safe house, and we would often host other kids who were in no shape to be seen by their parents. The only actual requirement was that every person who entered our house had to make eye contact and say hello to my parents. I had smart parents, huh? My mother was also a fantastic cook. I warned my friends that the food was great, but they had better dish out a compliment early on *before* my mother asked them what they thought of the meal. I cannot tell you how many times she threatened not to cook if we were not appreciative enough of her culinary talents. Playing cards in my house was an event. My parents were avid card players—bridge, pinochle, and whist—so when friends came over to play, they were like sharks circling chum ready to attack when a wrong card was played.

I have so many happy memories in that house, but there were also incidents that scarred me. Some severe punishments would not be tolerated in today's world. The yelling and chaos in our house were deafening at times, and the expectations were extremely high. Having a genius older brother did not bode well for my middle brother and me, who had shoes we would never be able to fill, at least academically. Somewhere around middle school, I started believing I was just not smart enough. Not-enoughness comes in all shapes and sizes for people, but mine was focused on not being smart enough or pretty enough.

Everyone thinks that enoughness is driven by external factors such as your job or financial status, your looks and intelligence, your standing in the community, and so on. Still, what I have learned through my own life and self-exploration, therapy, being coached, and my research is that we are never going to believe we are enough if we don't believe it from the inside out.

There is no amount of external validation that will cure the void inside of you without doing work on yourself.

I am unsure if my not-enoughness correlates to the sexual abuse I endured as a child, but how could it not have been a contributing factor? Active predators were in my neighborhood. I never discussed it with the other females in the neighborhood, but I would not be surprised if I was not the only one affected.

One perpetrator was a "babysitter," who exposed himself to me. I 1,000 percent remember telling my parents I did not want this person to watch me, but I know this fell on deaf ears. And, the other person was a much older neighbor who used to be my partner in hide-and-seek. But, it really became hide-and-touch. Much like other survivors discuss, I thought I was special. I did not realize this was not supposed to happen on any level. Maybe I had an inkling when I got older, but I cannot recall how often this happened or how old I was. I also don't remember when or why it stopped, although I can describe the exact spot where it took place. Memories are funny things—fuzzy and specific at the same time.

I guess it is no surprise that I felt unsafe. Who wouldn't in an environment where there was yelling, some hitting, overall mood unpredictability, financial worry, and abuse? I am not a therapist, but this seems like fertile ground for the seeds of not-enoughness to flourish. I "self-soothed" for far too long. Most kids stopped sucking their thumbs or using baby blankets long before I did. I wish I could remember how much money my parents paid me as a "reward" to get me to stop. I can always find the silver lining in things.

When I was in middle school, my mother was diagnosed with terminal breast cancer. While I was developing into a woman, she was losing a part of her femininity, so we were a little at odds during a time already loaded with mother-daughter tension. But, oh, how I loved my mother. My world revolved around her, and I have missed her presence every single day of my life. She lost her battle with breast cancer in my early twenties, right after my college graduation and two weeks after my brother, Matthew's, wedding. Her will to live for these events still inspires awe in me.

At one of her many hospital stays, the doctors would not let her come home unless she could put a tube in her nose down through her throat. I would never be able to do that, not in a million years. But once my mother decided to do something, there was no stopping her.

As teenage girls are programmed to do, I regularly went shopping with my best friend, Beth. She bought a skirt that she was unsure about. I thought my mother would validate this excellent fashion choice. Beth tried on the skirt and walked into my mother's room. My mother said, "Beth, that skirt is horrible on you! You have bigger hips, and the pockets accentuate them." I was mortified. On a funnier fashion note, she bought a T-shirt with "True" on one side of her chest and "False" on the other because people constantly looked to see if they could figure out which breast was real.

I survived high school with a few boyfriends and reasonably good grades. College was uneventful, except for my first true love. There is no way to describe him other than he was the epitome of a bad boy. He was my boss at a local restaurant I waitressed at, and he was quite a bit older than me. He was very successful, and I felt lucky to be in his presence. This is when not-enoughness really shines—in your relationships with people who have no business being in your orbit.

I know some of this sounds horrific, but it has shaped the person I am today. What I am enormously proud of is that I am incredibly resilient, strong, loyal, intelligent, and scrappy. And I am more than enough.

This is what I see in many of my clients—a lack of belief in themselves that hides under deep layers. The layers are so deep that this lack of confidence can make your most irrational and emotionally charged thoughts seem entirely reasonable. You are a master storyteller. You spend so much time in your head thinking about the what-ifs and what was that you cannot tell truth from fiction.

This is the purpose of my book. To tell my truth with the hope that I can help you find yours.

Babysitting, Books, Shoes and French Fries: The early working years

Where else does one start to work other than babysitting other kids in the neighborhood?

I remember getting fifty cents for thirty minutes watching two children while the mother picked up her husband at the train station. I had a mad crush on the father, a Boston lawyer. We shared a love of reading, and one day he loaned me a book I needed to read for school—*Rebecca*. What a book. I returned the book the next day, and I remember him being shocked that I had read it so quickly. I liked this type of attention! I have always been able to read fast, which has served me well.

Babysitting gave way to my first job at a shoe store after I got my license. The first car I drove was more powerful than a rocket and larger than my son's first apartment in New York City. It was a blue V-8 Mercury Grand Marquis, and I drove it during the gas crises of the late '70s. As my mother used to say, the gas needle moved just going down the street. It is here where I met one of my lifelong best friends, Cindy Guiness, who was also my first boss. I loved working in the shoe store, helping customers select the perfect shoe, ringing up sales, organizing shoes, and meeting new people. Maybe that is where I developed my current shoe obsession?

I was either not making enough money and/or not working enough hours, so I also got a job at Friendly's restaurant right across the street from the shoe store. I loved serving food and eating French fries and fribbles on breaks. My manager came up to me and told me I was a top seller for adding a side of fries to my sales. It didn't ever feel like selling because who doesn't want a side of Friendly's crinkly crispy fries with their meals? This really shaped my philosophy on sales. Selling should feel like you are providing something that someone wants or needs.

We had a communal tip jar that was to be divided evenly among all the servers at the end of the week. Two employees did some double-dipping with the tips but were eventually found out. I know this situation was remedied because a new process was put in place, but the fact that two people stole from the communal tip jar has stayed with me for over forty years. I became less trusting and more aware of my surroundings after this experience.

The University Book Store

My parents did not have a lot of money, so I was able to secure work during college. I got one of the best gigs on campus during my first year at the university bookstore. I thought I had died and gone to heaven. I had so many lovely things around me and everything I needed for school at a discount. I am positive that on more than one occasion, I spent more money than I made.

I met the cutest guy at the store who asked me on my first official college date. It became evident at dinner that he was much older than me when he referenced being in the war. I shriveled up at this point, but I still remember the best kiss and no future dates. We remained friends, and I can still recall his warm, smiling face and receding hairline.

I liked working at the store, and I loved my department manager. She liked me and gave me good hours. But I could not escape my mother's illness, which was becoming more aggressive. I went home quite a bit to spend time with her and my bad boy boyfriend. One of the requirements at the store was that you had to work one Saturday a month, and I did not meet this obligation. The store manager, who I can also readily picture, was not a huge fan of mine, and she was on to me. You had to be invited back to the store for the following year, and I was not invited back. My first work rejection hurt, but I earned it. From this experience, I learned that you must show up and follow the rules, even if you don't like them—seems simple.

Internships

Internships are a necessity for securing your post-college first job. I was a marketing major and had a great internship with a professor during the semester. But I also needed to find an internship over the summer between my junior and senior years. My dad pulled a few strings, and I got a coveted gig at an advertising agency in Boston's Back Bay. I got the bug for advertising agency life early on, and I spent most of my career in this space. I don't regret any of this for a second.

I learned the meaning of overtime, being on time, follow-up, and organization. And, because I wanted to work this into a full-time job after college, I put my hours in and then some. My hard work paid off, and eventually, I was offered my first full-time job for a whopping $14,500 a year. I negotiated the extra $500 for transportation into the city. I was so proud of myself.

I had accepted a computer sales job before the full-time position became available at the agency. The computer company wanted me to drive to and from Springfield, which was about an hour from my house, regularly without a mileage reimbursement. For the money they were paying me, I knew this would not work. Even in my early twenties, I knew something was amiss, and I declined the offer and waited until the ad agency had a full-time role. I don't remember this whole scenario very clearly, but I remember the hiring manager saying that many of the new hires had worked over the summer for free, which I didn't think was even legal.

Listening to my gut has been one of my greatest skills in life.

Adulting

My mom died on my first full-time day of work.

There is no way for me to write about my work experience and not mention this difficult tidbit. I still remember coming back from bereavement leave on the same day my co-worker returned from her vacation. I can still see the look of shock on her face. This group became my dysfunctional family. I had a cavernous void in my life that my work filled up.

My Entry-Level Role as an Account Coordinator

What a thankless job. When I started working in advertising, we did not have fax machines or computers, and we worked via phone and typing. If a client needed to see an ad proof, we used courier services. So many late nights, so many phone calls, and the fact that I was not great at typing but had to take ad copy via the phone is laughable when I look back on it. My client relationship skills had to kick in hard because I needed to compensate for my lack of typing skills.

The camaraderie of the late nights and the agency antics were irreplaceable, and I am still friends with many of my co-workers and clients from this time. Who would have thought the invention of the fax would drastically change my life? In the beginning, those babies took six minutes to send one page. I couldn't wait for the internet to get here; it sure did a few years later.

I noticed my working habits seemed to set me apart from many of my peers. I wanted to work and be loaded up with clients, learn and grow, and know everything as soon as possible. Patience has never been a virtue of mine, but I continue to work on it!

The woman next to me dawdled about and moved at such a glacial pace. I knew I would surpass her. Agency life has high turnover, but I wanted to stay, get promoted, and hang with the cooler, more senior kids. They made me work for this, but I eventually got there! I worked hard and rose up to become a coveted account executive. Barely five feet tall and one-hundred pounds, I was ready to sell our services to anyone who needed them.

Boys Ruin Everything

As was the fairly traditional cycle at the time, you got your first job and moved out of your childhood home, which meant leaving my poor widowed dad behind. Then you are on a mission to meet your life partner. After meeting quite a few toads, I finally met the father of my children. He was a client, so it was not something I was completely comfortable with. We tried to cover things up, but eventually, the cat was out of the proverbial bag.

He got a job in another city, and I moved with him because we were newly engaged. If you feel sadness and hesitation, you are correct. Leaving this crazy place and my built-in support system was devastating to me. But I went and began my next job search and my new life.

From New Jersey, we went to Pittsburgh, then to the Philadelphia area, and then back again to the Boston area after our son was born. Three years later, our daughter was born. These were uneventful working years as we were chasing my then-husband's dream, not my own. Throughout my life, I often believed I could not have any of my own dreams because I was so caught up in helping the people around me—sad but true.

I worked throughout the time my kids were young because, despite supporting my husband's career moves, I must have had the instinct to work to survive. And I generally liked to work. Had I not stayed in the workforce, I would have been in far different circumstances when I had to raise and support my children on my own.

I don't want to dwell on the negative here about my ex, but he had some significant mental health and addiction challenges that interfered with his ability to find and keep a job. I had resigned myself to staying in the marriage to keep my family together. But my son had an incident with two other boys at a day camp where one of the mothers said she felt like she needed to call an attorney to protect herself from my husband. This was the final straw, and I finally decided to leave my husband and my ill-fated dreams of a fairy tale life.

Ironically, my mother-in-law had found an addiction therapist for her and me to see because things had deteriorated at home. We even went to an Al-Anon meeting together. I did everything possible to try to save my marriage, and I believe my ex did too. He was unwell, though, and I realized I couldn't save him. I had to save myself for my kids. I had to save myself. My therapist said, "When you started therapy, you were hopeful about your marriage. By the end, you were hopeless."

During our marriage, I was in sales, and I was very successful. This helped me gain the courage to know I could handle life as a single mother. As part of the divorce settlement, I had to pay him half of my 401(k) and stock options and buy him out of half the house. Financially, being a working mother didn't work in my favor, but I earned my freedom, and I was relieved, happy, and proud.

My marriage was never good—not from the first second we got married. We certainly had some good times, but the bad times outweighed the good by a long shot. I don't regret this marriage because, without it and him, I would not have my most amazing children.

For others reading this, know I see you, I feel you, and I was you. There is life on the other side.

CHAPTER 2

DO YOU WEAR A MASK?

"Masking is a process in which humans change or 'mask' their natural personality to conform to social norms or conventional 'expected' behaviors. This term was first used to describe the act of concealing disgust by Ekman (1972) and Friesen (1969)."

—IFIQUE.COM, N.D.

I kept a stockpile of masks right by the door of my house so I wouldn't forget to wear one whenever I went out, which was not often during COVID-19. Generally, I also kept several in my car for the same reason. Our town was an early adopter of mask-wearing. Early in the pandemic, when masks were not yet mandatory, I drove to Starbucks to pick up my latte. I immediately noticed I had forgotten mine, and there was not a mask to be found in my car where I usually kept a sizable stash. I immediately turned around and drove home because I did not want to walk into a local store and not have a mask on.

At work and in my life outside of work, I thought of myself as a chameleon, changing my behavior to accommodate who I was with and what the situation called for. I saw this adaptability as my superpower because being able to read a room was critical for my success as a salesperson and a leader.

I know I also wore masks in my personal life because who doesn't want to fit in? I was often aware of the switch, and I could feel myself changing colors and preparing for whatever was required. Other times, I knew I was on autopilot, and my mask went on without thought. Defense mechanisms are highly effective tools.

But holy heck, when I forgot my mask on the way to Starbucks, I felt so exposed. I went for a walk earlier that week at my favorite outdoor spot and ran into some friends wearing masks. They didn't say anything to me, but I was ashamed because I did not have a mask on. The mask-wearing guidance was all over the place in the early stages. But, to be honest, the deeper issue was the potential for embarrassment. What if someone I knew saw me without a mask? What if word got around that Donna Star was an anti-mask wearer? Wow, do we tell ourselves stories.

We, or certainly I, have this compulsive need to keep ourselves safe and free from criticism. We go to great lengths to keep our masks on. This can show up as not speaking up when disagreeing with someone, agreeing with someone when you don't agree, or going along to get along.

This can and often does come at a significant personal cost to you. I have heard this statement that I completely agree with, "Keeping the peace with others can cause a war within you."

I have always had a good sense of humor. I like to laugh. I genuinely like to smile. And I like to make people laugh and smile. I had a client meeting in my early years with a large defense contractor. It was a very formal environment and getting in the building was like getting into Ft. Knox. Anyway, I finally got a meeting here with the top decision maker. The meeting was about how we would manage the

As I stated earlier in this chapter, I thought my super-power was my adaptability, and maybe it still is. But today, that adaptability is not at my expense. I am not hiding my anger, feelings, or words just to fit in—to go along and get along. I am also leaning into my new superpower of creating. I am creating the life I want, creating the work I want to do and the people I want to work with, creating this book, creating programs, and creating for creation's sake. Allowing creativity to happen is a gift because we so often squelch it.

When Lightning Strikes

I am not a storm chaser. Lightning is a natural phenom-enon—beautiful and powerful and best experienced from afar. Recently, there was a story in the news about a car that got hit by lightning. I didn't think that was possible. I remember from my childhood hearing that the rubber on tires kept cars safe.

Unless you are a weather person, you likely don't know where and when lightning will strike. This is precisely how great ideas can happen. Have you ever just been hanging around, and poof, a great idea pops into your head? Or, you could be doing just about anything, and this same thing happens. In fact, just like lightning, we use the phrase that an idea *struck* us. Here is the definition of inspiration: *Inspiration occurs spontaneously, without intention.*

I created F.E.M.A.L.E. at my desk on my birthday during COVID-19. This a program for early-career women who have gotten their first or second jobs but have not been trained on life—promotions, work politics, roommate issues, and all the stuff that we assume this group of people knows because they don't. One week after I thought of the idea, I executed and started running the group.

I have discovered that community helps when people realize they are not alone. I want people to become more present and know they have much more agency over their lives. Currently, they may be choosing to not use their voices and/or assume and accept that stress is just part of a busy life. They decide to take themselves so seriously because that is what they have been taught.

A need and want for a deeper connection is always there. I attended a three-day retreat at Kripalu, which is one of the US's preeminent yoga and mindfulness centers. When asked why we participated in the workshop, overwhelmingly, all of us wanted to reclaim ourselves and connect to others.

We tend to hold back what we really feel. We all do. We all want approval, even if we aren't aware of it. And it is slowly killing us on the inside. You don't say the things you want to say because of the what-ifs—I upset someone, I get fired, I am wrong, I am judged for being an idiot, and so on. I think we have all been there at some point. Am I right? Yes, I am!

I also created SILII, a group program for mid- to senior-level career women because community is important at every stage of work and life. SILII stands for Say It Like It Is with the double meaning of being silly. The weight of expectations is so incredibly heavy. And, with this heaviness, we can lose our levity. I see it every day with clients regardless of gender. All the stuff we are supposed to do, say, and act. It is exhausting. This program creates a place where people can breathe, connect, and share. The program has a very light curriculum—just humans interacting with other good humans under the safe and watchful eye of an executive coach.

Here is data to support simply having fun at work:

Fact: organizations in which humor is part of the culture reported shareholder returns 19 percent higher than their competitors, according to a Huet & Associates study. Humor connects people and encourages them to be present —hence the group! Injecting humor and levity in our daily work interactions, even virtually, can change how our brains work, generating more alpha brainwaves that help us develop creative solutions, reduce stress, and solve problems. Most importantly, it builds resiliency, which can help employees better navigate the challenges and changes we are regularly facing and bounce back more quickly (Horning 2021).

I understand that we have to act respectfully and read the rooms we are in, but that is not what is holding us back. We buy into the belief system that we must be everything we have been told we need to be—responsible, earning a living, taking care of our families, working on that promotion, and so on. Where is taking care of yourself in this equation? And why do you all think you are selfish for taking care of yourself? You are not.

Although I don't think of myself as particularly creative, I have created three group coaching programs. I have a waiting list for my one-on-one coaching. I write biweekly emails. I write regularly on LinkedIn. I have taken additional courses, including Neuroscience for Business through MIT. And I wrote this book. I guess this makes me more creative than I realized.

All this "creativity" was inside me long before I left my corporate job, but I didn't have the time, energy, or confidence to allow myself to create. I could name all the reasons why and you would believe them—single mother, crazy corporate job, travel, taking care of the house/kids, trying to have a life. They are all plausible and partially true.

Excuses are the lies we tell ourselves to keep us exactly where we are.

I know you also have great ideas. But we often let these ideas pass because they come in so fast and fleetingly. I don't do that anymore. There is gold in these thoughts. So, I challenge you to capture that lightning in a bottle and write down your next idea. Then go ahead and execute it!

I will continue doing the same. Could there be a book number two in my future?

CHAPTER 3

WHEN YOUR COMPANY IS YOUR CO-PARENT

"How can you not write about your divorce since you are writing about your corporate career? Your company became our co-parent."

—JORDAN STAR, MY TWENTY-NINE-YEAR-OLD SON

I started Googling to see what had been written about bringing company cultures into the home. Clearly, I was not alone. I stumbled on an article in *Forbes* about adult children of workaholics (ACOW). I didn't even know this term existed. As is the case when you start Googling, you go down a lot of rabbit holes.

Let's start with a description of workaholism. Workaholism is the best-dressed addiction that camouflages the underlying addiction for everyone in the family. Yet, according to research, adults with a workaholic parent carry psychological scars that they are often unaware of. Children of workaholics often grow into adults envied by everyone—responsible, achievement-oriented, and able to take charge of any situation. At least, that's how they appear to the outside world. Inside, they often feel like little kids who can never do anything right, holding themselves up mercilessly to standards of perfection (Robinson 2021).

I suppose this is not much different than the "you are the company you keep" phrase. For me, it illustrates just a little bit more awareness that my son understood at a very deep level that I was not only taking my work home, but I was taking the culture home too.

He told me that other people, including our friends and family, would look at him with a knowing glance about my behavior. Apparently, I didn't switch over to parent mode easily enough, and I stayed in boss mode longer than I should have. I wanted peak efficiency at home. Homework done check, showers done check, dinner ready check, prepared for whatever activities are coming up check, playdates check. I wanted my home to run like a well-oiled machine, except my children are human beings, not machines.

Here is one of my most cringe-worthy, you took your work home with you to an extreme extent, funny, but not in a good way, stories. My son was in middle school, and he came home with a not-great mid-term report. When I saw the report, I was not happy. I put my son on a PIP, which means performance improvement plan in the corporate world.

I sat with him, asked him a series of questions, and set out to have him build a plan to improve his grades.

"Ask your teachers what you need to do to raise your grades."
"What is the highest grade you can achieve if you do all of the work required?"
"Is there extra credit work available?"

forms. My ex had issues with alcohol, and I had issues with work. It helps me to know that I am not alone, and my children are not alone. We all have childhood trauma to overcome to become the best versions of ourselves.

I was focused on not having to worry about money because my family had financial insecurity growing up. When I was maybe ten or eleven, the electric company came to our front door asking for money or they would shut off our electricity. The electricity was shut off, and I know my mother was angry and devastated. Eventually, the lights came back on, but the embarrassment of this memory has not dimmed. I went some holidays without gifts and rode the same blue banana seat bike around town despite my dad's empty promise that I would soon have a new bike. This was my mode of transportation around town, and I was on my bike every day in the summer, riding to and from the town lake and to my friends' houses. I must have been in very good shape.

My ex-husband came from a wealthy family, and I was somewhat unconsciously attracted to him because maybe he would be able to fill this hole of financial insecurity. He had a strong mother, who I still love to this day, and two sisters. I had no sisters and a deceased mother, so our pairing seemed like a dream come true. I thought he was a complete match for what was missing in me. But wounds and attachments are much more profound than beginning relationships' superficial nature. His mental health, which apparently was not a secret to his mother and family, was not fully disclosed to me. His mom had brought him to a therapist earlier in his life because she knew something was amiss, but she was told she was being a hysterical mother. I feel for her because a mom always knows.

I want to break the cycle of allowing my kids' trauma to dictate and impact their adult life as much as is possible. Is it too late? Neither has had a meaningful relationship that I know of, and I don't seem very close to a grandchild yet. My daughter is on the right path with solid boundaries and a healthy and productive work ethic. My son is a wildly creative thinker and is forging his own way. He created a clothing brand, Bubuleh, during COVID-19. No, I wasn't ecstatic that he quit his marketing job with benefits, but why not? He has no mortgage, no kids, and no one to support other than himself. I am really proud of both of them. Time will tell. Love will tell. Life will tell. Hopefully, they have the support, love, and professional help to live their most beautiful lives possible.

Regardless of our challenges, we did a lot right. I did a lot right. Over the years, I've spent considerable time thinking about the scars my children have because of their childhood. What will they take with them when they have families of their own? I am glad that we have been able to talk about their experiences. I hope it is healing for them.

My family calls me Donna 2.0 because I have so vastly changed from my corporate years of hard driving, hard-charging, sharp criticism, and never-enough mentality to a much more thoughtful human. My daughter told me in our interview that "you listen more intently now, something I wished you had done a better job of in my childhood." Our kids' truths as they see them can hurt us, heal us, and help us in so many ways if we let them. But it still wasn't easy to hear.

By leaving my corporate job, becoming a certified executive coach, and hiring coaches for myself, I have made tremendous progress in moving away from being a workaholic. If you are ready, ask yourself some tough questions.

How can you heal your workaholism?

- What would you feel like if you lost your job tomorrow?
- Is your identity and sense of self-worth tied up in your profession/job title/status? You are clearly not alone if the answer is yes.
- If you knew today was your last day on earth, are you doing everything you have ever wanted to do?
- When is enough enough?

I realize that the cure for workaholism might seem difficult because you have never done it any other way. But, if you want to see your children grow up, spend more time with loved ones, and not expire in your chair because you feel the need to show everyone how hard you work, then you have taken the first step by realizing there is more to life than work.

My ex-husband and I went to counseling early in our marriage because I thought he had a drinking problem. He made me feel like I had the problem because I was too sensitive about what was very commonplace.

I remember the therapist saying very clearly, "If you think your husband has a problem, then it is a problem."

This simple statement meant everything to me because I was convinced the issue was mine.

Don't disregard your own feelings.

What advice do I have to help you get to the other side? Here are some quick thoughts:

- Acknowledge you have a problem. I know I _____ too much, and as a result, I miss important things in my life.
- Pay attention to what your loved ones are saying to you. If they genuinely love you, then maybe what they say is valid.
- Acknowledge if you really want to change. Lip service to your loved ones without actual change can worsen the situation and increase overall frustration.
- Talk to someone you trust because making changes is much harder to do alone.
- Start small. What can you do that will feel manageable?
  - Shut down an hour earlier one night of the week.
  - Pick a day or two to start work later in the day and have breakfast with your wife/kids/partner/yourself.
  - Schedule one fun activity on your calendar. It can be for thirty minutes.
  - Start small (worth repeating).
  - Set realistic expectations for yourself and those affected by your schedule.
  - Revisit if you feel any different in your body at the end of a few weeks. See if people around you notice any changes.
  - Be true to your word.
  - Recognize your accomplishments of making small changes. They lead to bigger changes over time.

Being a workaholic isn't really all about work. It is about your self-worth.

You feel alive when you are busy, challenged, needed, productive, driving results, and successful. It is a drug like no other. Once you actively try to consume less work and participate more in your life, you may feel more confident. You may start to see your life more fully. You may begin to enjoy your life outside of work more.

I may be dating myself here, but the scene in *Pretty Woman* where Richard Gere takes off his shoes and feels the green grass on his bare feet says it all. He was such a workaholic; he didn't even realize what other gifts the world had to share with him. A cold drink and a hot dog while lying on the green grass on a beautiful, hot sunny day. You can see the sheer joy on his face. I can feel it too.

I hope this will be the case for you. I hope you find a more balanced life, your whole sense of self is not tied to your work, and you realize you are so much more than your paycheck, title, material goods, and status.

You are so much more.

CHAPTER 4

SHOULD I STAY, OR SHOULD I GO?

"You don't spend enough time being my mom."

My son was eight years old when he said that to me. Eventually, it prompted me to leave my job at my old company. I went to a local media buying company in the same town where I lived so there would be less travel, and I would be closer to home. I left after a few short months because I was bored, didn't work well with the owners, and did not like the media-buying industry.

When I gave my notice again a few years later, the company found a better position for me. I had a new boss, who was intolerable. He could go on for hours about sales funnels and the like, but I never saw him sell anything or develop a good relationship with a client, or another employee, for that matter. I have never spent so much wasted time on phone calls. It is 1,000,000 percent true that people leave bosses, not companies. I knew without a doubt he was trying to replace me right after he started. I was not wrong.

When I left to start my own business, I was tired and burned out. I had a friend who was the CEO of an IT consulting firm who offered me consulting work to provide a soft landing for my departure. Everyone in my life knew I needed a change. So, my idea was to consult for companies who needed help in evaluating sales, HR, and recruiting areas because this was my background. My first consulting gig was reviewing the sales organization's effectiveness from top to bottom—pricing, people, and process. I did this for another firm and then another.

The work was labor intensive, and I did not have the chops to act like a consultant. I got too invested in the companies I worked for, and I did not see enough of my recommended changes being implemented. I did not have a business plan, a website, or a sales and marketing strategy. I am not saying you need all these things, but for me, I just didn't feel ready enough to be on my own. I ended up returning to my old company again in a great new position. At the same time, a close colleague of mine was diagnosed with terminal cancer. The timing was right and felt important.

I am a very proud Bostonian and, by default, a diehard Patriots fan, which let me weave a tale about how similar my story is to Tom Brady's. Who would have thought my life and Tom's had so much in common?

Be like Tom (Brady)

Several years ago, if you had told me Tom Brady would not end his career as a Patriot, I would have thought you were crazy! Boston has always had a complete love fest with Tom Brady—six Super Bowl wins and an entire Patriot nation dedicated to his every whim. There's *no* way he is not ending his career here. We bleed Boston sports and use Larry Bird as our yardstick; you don't leave this town because we have a completely wonderful symbiotic relationship. Why would anyone want to leave *Boston?* Yankees fans need not respond.

But, when I heard Tom Brady was, in fact, leaving Boston, I paused and thought, it is time. This staying/leaving discussion is too much of a distraction, and we have gotten more than we ever hoped for out of this relationship. Then, I heard Cam Newton would be our next quarterback, and I thought, yes! Not everyone agreed with me, and they were right, but the Patriots have long been a team of second chances. It doesn't always work out, but hey, we try. With Cam's talent and athleticism and a one-year contract, I truly believed this was a perfect fit for Cam and the Patriots. Side note: Even more than winning—well, almost—I enjoyed the joy I saw on Cam's face after each winning play. We didn't often see that with Brady because he was so intent on winning the game and proving his maniacal focus.

Okay, but how on God's green earth can I weave this back to coaching, you ask? Hold my beer/wine.

Sometimes, it is time to go even when everything has been award-winning crazy good. Even when you have more money and status than you could have ever hoped for, even when you have adoring fans and a loving family, you know deep in your body and soul it is time to go. You want to continue to grow. You want new challenges.

Very often, people ignore these signals. People often think leaving means there is anger, ruin, and frustration, but sometimes the complete opposite is true. For me, I knew it was time to leave my corporate career. I could have stretched it out further, but I wanted to be fair to my employer, my teams, my clients, and myself. I wanted to do as little harm as possible because my career, relationships, and legacy mattered to me. Surely, you see that Tom and I have much in common!

Now, I have no real way of knowing what went on behind the scenes with all the negotiations, but I know I am grateful for Tom and all he has done for this city, although I was bitter in the beginning. He has a killer competitive streak and wanted to continue to prove himself. And, in *much* warmer weather. Good for you, Tom. I, now, wish you well.

By the way, happy retirement for real this time!

Please tell me that you are a fan of Ted Lasso—spoiler alert ahead—the Apple+ show about an American coach who knows nothing about soccer coaches a team in the UK. It is a glorious show that strikes right at your feel-good heart and touches on tough topics such as mental health in sports. Keeley, the team's PR representative, gave her best friend and boss her notice because she was offered a fantastic opportunity to start her own PR agency. There was no bad blood. Good mentors and great leaders know you are going to leave someday. And they leave the door open should you ever want to return. Keeley didn't struggle with her decision because she knew it was the right move, as did her boss, Rebecca.

Don't confuse sad feelings with wrong choices.

I have been running a corporate leadership development program with another coach for over two years now. But we both decided it was time to move on. Our businesses have evolved. I am sure it had been on her mind as well as mine, but I finally decided to say it to her before we had hard feelings toward each other. Leaving a situation doesn't have to be contentious, especially if you get in front of it before things really turn sour. Who wants all that negativity in their lives?

When I left my corporate job for the final time, I was ready to go, and my company was ready for me to leave. There were no burned bridges. I was ready to face and answer the question constantly rattling around in my head "What am I here on this earth to do?"

These conversations you have inside your head are on a constant loop—should I stay or go in this relationship, should I stay or go with this job, and on and on. We all do it—every single one of us. You may not realize at the time how much energy this takes out of you. If only indecision burned calories instead of brain cells.

If you believe in the premise that there are no mistakes in life:

> What would you do if you knew that nothing bad was going to happen to you?
> What steps would you take to create the life you really want?
> What do you need to resolve for you to believe in yourself enough to finally take action?

Let's take a step back and really identify what inaction/limbo means and feels like. Limbo is a state that includes uncertainty, unknowing, and a lack of clarity. And it is perfectly normal. The COVID-19 years have been hard on everyone.

An excerpt from *Psychology Today:*

> The American Psychological Association's "Stress in America" report from March 2022 showed that we have been suffering from mental exhaustion due to the prolonged and unrelenting uncertainty in our lives during the past two years.

The 3,012 adults polled reported how the impact of prolonged stress has been wearing them down: "Americans have been doing their best to persevere over these past two tumultuous years, but these data suggest that we're now reaching unprecedented levels of stress that will challenge our ability to cope."

Living in the grip of "When will the other shoe fall off?" or "When will this ever end?" for two years is not what humans are wired to handle. Prolonged Limbo and uncertainty affect us differently than short-term periods of putting our lives on hold. An APA report from late 2021 showed how we are having difficulty making decisions and planning ahead, let alone keeping commitments, because our lives keep changing so quickly. More than half of adults (56 percent) in March 2022 "reported experiencing a relationship strain or end" (Walker 2022).

These are undoubtedly unprecedented times. While living in limbo is not new, many of the above events are outside our control. What about if you are living in limbo and it is in your control? You are living in limbo because you are unwilling to deal or feel with some aspect of your life. You can decide whether to leave a job, leave a relationship, or leave a friendship.

Staying in limbo is a decision you make. Indecision is a decision.

When a coaching client comes to me and says they don't know or are confused as to why they stay, the reality is that they always know the answer. It may be buried deep inside them, and more than likely, it has a lot of pain or shame associated with the answer.

The discussions in your brain may go something like this:

"If I leave, I will never meet anyone again."
"My kids will hate me."
"What will the neighbors/my friends/my family think?"
"I should just stick it out."

Thus, you have decided to stay, but the dialogue in your head is not going away because the situation is not resolved.

Let's jump into what a work discussion might sound like:

"I am well paid."
"I will never find another job that pays me as much as this one."
"I have to support my family."
"I have no right to look elsewhere."
"I should be happy."
"My work situation is not *that* bad."

I think I have said each one of these sentences to myself and to others. These "conversations" in our heads keep us exactly where we are. But there is hope—lots and lots of hope.

Once you realize you are sabotaging your life by not acting, you can make different choices. I work with a brilliant financial professional who has had an incredible career. He started his career at one of the premier financial services organizations. He is divorced and remarried to the "love of his life," and they recently had their second child. He needs to find a new job for a variety of reasons, but there are so many stories in his head, such as his best days are behind him, he is unclear on what he wants to do next, he doesn't want to let down his family, and so on. And, he has lost some confidence in his abilities.

Our work together happens on multiple fronts. I coach the person, not the situation. If I start working on his résumé and networking, I am missing what makes him tick, and he is the critical component to his success. He must believe in himself to give himself the boost to start networking and talking to and about himself more positively. This is not toxic positivity—believing the best in yourself exists even though your negative thoughts are barking at you on a constant loop—even though life has thrown you some curveballs.

Once we acknowledged and validated the emotional turmoil he was going through, he was able to move on. He has made tremendous progress and is currently in talks with two exceptional companies.

I can tell where a client, who is mulling the idea of a job switch, is at mentally by asking one simple question. "How comfortable are you with networking?" More comfortable people might say, "I love to network." Less comfortable people might say, "I haven't connected with people in my network for a while. They will think it is weird when I reach out to them."

Of course, there are many other possible responses, but this gives me an idea of what you may need from coaching. I have absolutely no judgment. We just need a starting point to be the most effective. I also realize for more introverted people, networking may be way out of your comfort zone. I don't discount this, but for a solid job search, networking is one of the most effective ways to find your next job.

The hiring process isn't called the "black hole of recruiting" because it is easy and efficient. I want to help you stack the deck in your favor. Former colleagues, friends, and relatives all want to help you find your best next job. They do.

In some cases, I can see that my clients who are looking for jobs are self-sabotaging.

One client came to me because she wanted a promotion at her company and had been there for over ten years. She had applied for a position the previous year and did not get the job. I asked her to tell me about the interview. She spent the next ten minutes telling me how she went about the interview. She told them what she didn't know about the role, and she was poking her nose in to say she was interested, but she likely did not have the correct experience.

She 1,000 percent set herself up to *not* get this job. When I relayed what I heard, she said, "yes, in the interview, I did not sell myself into the job, I sold myself out of it." Before I work with her on how to position herself for her next career move, we need to dig in and figure out why she is more comfortable selling herself out than in. With the same level of experience as another candidate, she will not get a job with this approach.

Another question I may ask when you are in limbo:

"What would be the worst-case scenario if you took action?"

You won't get the job if you don't apply, and that is for sure. You won't get the bump in salary unless you ask. If you don't ask, you don't receive. People tend to catastrophize the worst possible outcome. Lose a job today, homeless tomorrow. Laid off or exited, you will never again work in your industry. But there are many steps in between. Once I get a client to start here, we can add some relief to the worst-case scenario topics that rarely, if ever, happen.

I am no different than any of my clients. I stayed in my corporate job for far too long. The underlying reason is because I just didn't believe in myself enough. I was finally ready to change that.

My children are, without question, the most important people in my life. I was a single mom starting when my children were three and six. Their father loved them deeply, but had his own challenges and died far too soon when they were in high school and college, respectively. Their life was not easy. I wanted and needed to provide for them. The story I told myself was that I couldn't leave because they needed me to provide for them and looking for another job was irresponsible.

I lived in limbo land. Do you live there too?

We were fortunate with our caregivers who became part of our family. We had nannies so I could move about the country freely and ensure they were taken care of. I have very little guilt about this aspect of child rearing because I am in the camp that the more people who love your children, the better.

I firmly support the research that highlights that a good nanny can have a positive effect on a child's cognitive and social development. Younger children experience less stress when receiving quality childcare at home. And, when a child's caregiver is warm, sensitive, and positively engaged, young kids benefit (SPNannies, 2019).

I learned a lot more about myself in my Coach Training Program and the limits I self-imposed on myself. I didn't build any real learning time into my corporate life, so I was very nervous about the learning required in the program. A lot of prework was required. My body went into shock before the training started because I was so nervous I would not be able to keep up. Complete transparency was necessary and required. The whole experience has made me a better coach, person, mother, partner, family member, and friend.

Listening is at the heart of coaching. Not just listening to what is said but listening to what is not said—intuitive listening. It is like magic when you listen to someone, and they feel safe enough to open up to you and themselves.

A favorite quote:

> "Being heard is so close to being loved that for the average person, they are almost indistinguishable."
>
> —DAVID W. AUGSBURGER, *CARING ENOUGH TO HEAR AND BE HEARD* (2008)

I recently asked my daughter how my corporate career affected her. I was not ready for the onslaught of emotion that came out of this. Some of her friends' mothers did not work. No real surprise there, given the town we lived in. The positives were that she said she had more independence, but she thought I had limited attention to give her—Ugh.

Specifically, she said, "You did not have the patience to listen and were relatively closed off and crippled by stress. I was never sure which mom I would get when I got home from school."

On a more positive note, we had a village of people who loved us, and she was always loved and cared for. When she had the opportunity to introduce me to her college friends, she told them we did not have a traditional family. She always felt different because of her dad and our divorce.

She had a roommate who I adored during her sophomore year. Her roommate's father spent the weekend with her for father/daughter weekend. Hannah and her roommate got into his car, and her roommate's father asked, "How was your day?" Hannah relayed this conversation and said, "I never had this with Dad." This simple interchange with a father and daughter had just never happened.

I know she loved her dad, but he was a source of embarrassment for her. I understood this because, growing up, I was sometimes embarrassed by my dad. He owned his own painting contracting business and drove around town in a run-down truck in his well-worn painting clothes. Other parents I knew had more professional jobs. But he never missed a game or event that his three children or grandchildren had. He was a very present father, and I had the chance to move on from my initial embarrassment of him as I grew up and understood myself better. My daughter did not have this opportunity.

She remembers me saying, "Never do what I do for work." What I really meant was, "Don't work like me."

She could not understand what was more important than spending time with family. She didn't understand the purpose of the way I lived my life. I asked her if she ever saw me happy at work, and she said, "When you were in the office with your teams."

On my last day of work, she wrote this on Instagram:

"Happy last day of work to my kickass mama star. I can't believe this day has come, and I am inexplicably proud of and excited for you. No more late nights in the office or stressful meetings!! I know your work family will miss you, but your real fam is ready to celebrate with you. I'm not sure what this #rebrand will bring, but I'm so pumped to see chill star in action. You inspire me every day with your beauty, intelligence, humor, and class. Congrats to the biggest nugget boss lady there is!! It's time for a lemon drop."

She also developed a slogan right around the time I left work: "Phone off; Family on." We made magnets and coffee mugs and gave them as gifts on our family trip. To her, family is everything. Being present is everything and work is not.

Should I have left sooner? Yes. Do I wish I could have believed in myself earlier so my kids would see my transformation sooner? Also, yes. The key is that I made the change.

It is never too late to make the changes you desire.

CHAPTER 5

EVERY INCH COUNTS WHEN YOU DON'T BELIEVE YOU ARE ENOUGH

Measuring up!

All my life, I waited and waited and waited for a growth spurt. I come from a long line of short people, but I still hoped to rise out of this familial situation. I remember when I finally hit five feet tall, I was ecstatic because this was a massive accomplishment for a woman in my family. But this was short-lived. I started to compare myself to the other short people in my class, and I wasn't the shortest. I was in the average range of being short. There was one girl named Nina who was shorter than me. She was absolutely adorable with naturally straight blonde hair and green eyes. In short, she was the perfect short person. In my estimation, I did not measure up.

Interestingly enough, there is research to suggest that height does matter in your corporate career. Someone who is six feet tall earns, on average, nearly $166,000 more during a thirty-year career than someone who is five feet five inches—even when controlling for gender, age, and weight. In fact, in the workplace, each inch above average may be worth $789 more per year, according to a study in the *Journal of Applied Psychology* (Vol. 89, No. 3) (Dittman, 2004).

As I examine the root of "not being enough," oftentimes called a gremlin, I know the seeds were sown early in my childhood, as they often are. I couldn't even get short right. As you grow, or hope to, in my case, you see you aren't the prettiest, tallest, smartest, or coolest. You aren't generally the "est" at anything you are comparing yourself to. And, this not being enough has dogged me throughout my life, which is not to say I don't have a great life; it is just to say that when you live in comparison, you are very rarely on the winning side of that internal conversation.

I always attributed this feeling of not being enough *as the driving force* of my success, very commonly known as fear of failure. But as I dove deeper into coaching, I realized what a *crock* this thinking really is. Are you successful if all you are thinking about is failing? And, for those of you who don't buy into this, if you are worried about failing, do you ever truly celebrate your success? Part two of this thinking is that once you are successful, you think it can all be taken away, so you are never at peace. Are you with me here?

My first mentor coach asked to interview me on his weekly Facebook Live program because he considers me a successful coach. My gremlin went into high gear. Am I considered a successful coach? Surely, there are way more successful coaches out there. But I settled in and said to myself, "of course, there are more successful coaches out there, but you are also successful." The live event went very well.

Success isn't like pie; there is enough for everyone. I did not have this self-talk down earlier in my life, and it most certainly would have helped me. This work is ongoing because just when you think you have tamed your gremlin, it will find new ways to pop into your life. In my training program, we had to name and draw our gremlin and present it in our class, which caused more anxiety in the program than any other exercise. Nothing brings out your gremlin more than talking about your gremlin, but you cannot tame something that you don't acknowledge exists.

And, if you are truly plagued by not being enough as I have been, relaxing can wreak havoc on the brain.

The Downside of Downtime

For me, downtime has always been the enemy of productivity. If I wasn't busy, I wasn't valued. I certainly didn't value myself; the more flights a week and fires to put out, the better. I used to wish for downtime when I was in my corporate job, but when I went on vacation, it was not uncommon for me to get sick. Resting and relaxing put my body into a shock of some kind because I was so unused to this state of being. I looked into this, and I was gob smacked to learn there is an actual name for this, leisure sickness. Leisure sickness, as defined in a 2002 Dutch study, is "the condition of developing symptoms of sickness during weekends and/or vacations" (Brenza, 2017).

To be honest, I used to wish I would get sick so I could rest. I am talking about hospitalization sick. Apparently, I am not alone because when I shared this on LinkedIn, quite a few people shared that they felt the same way, which is not good. Even when I was ill, though, I worked anyway because what better way to feel valued than working through illness?

I went into labor while giving my largest client an office tour. By this time in my pregnancy, the walk from the parking lot to the office was daunting, as was the idea of putting on a nice outfit. Were my nice maternity outfits even clean? Did they still fit? I had just about grown out of all my maternity clothes and had to pee every twenty minutes or so. But the client was flying in from Kentucky, so I had no choice. It was an important visit for the client to meet their account team. Everyone was looking forward to this visit. It was my job to host, and as I introduced Jamie around the office, I started getting considerable pains. I made frequent stops at the desks we were visiting. I had not yet put together that I was having contractions. I had my beautiful baby girl, Hannah, the next day.

While working at home one day, a client called me while my daughter, who was probably not much more than a year old, was throwing up. I remember calmly walking Hannah over to the sink as she continued vomiting and stayed on the phone talking to my client. No, I did not win a mother of the year (MOY) award that day or year. The ridiculous thing is that I did it without thinking. It never really dawned on me that this was not freaking normal. None of this was normal.

I used to take Fridays off when my kids were young. This predated laptops and the twenty-four-hour connected lifestyle we are currently living in, but my clients had my home and cell phone numbers. One day while playing with my son in the basement, I heard the phone ring. I was not going to answer it, but my young son said, "Mom, it could be Kindred." Kindred was my largest account at that time. If he knew the name of the client, I must have talked about them at home quite a bit.

I left my corporate career before COVID-19 struck. For all those busy bees like myself, I know COVID-19 was a shock to the system. The world shut down and didn't reopen for a solid two years, depending on your profession. I know many people were busier working at home juggling both worlds simultaneously. This constant need to work and prove myself was a *me* issue, not a corporate issue. But companies do benefit from having workaholic employees, don't they?

As I sat in some much-needed reflection reviewing the previous year, I went through a long list of things I should have accomplished:

- I should have worked out more.
- I should have done more around the house.
- Why didn't I cook more?
- Why hadn't I organized my living spaces?

My list went on and on. I logged into Facebook and saw that I had done my first Facebook Live with PowerPoint in hand on this day several years earlier. I was scared to watch the replay because I was embarrassed about what I might have said or done, but I watched it anyway. It wasn't half bad, and that is when I started to turn the tide.

Holy moly, what progress I have made! I have literally built a successful coaching business in a little over three years—new clients, clients who have renewed with me, clients who have not, a new Corporate Leadership Accelerator Program for women, corporate workshops, group coaching programs, and now this book! Yes, I have moments when I am hard on myself, but they are not nearly as frequent or as intense as they once were.

Here is what I also do when my system is on anxiety overload.

I breathe.

Maybe this is too much information (TMI), but I also take hot baths. Some of my best social media posts come from here.

I sit in silence, forcing my brain just to shut off, and it is freeing.

One of my close friends once said I was "unmeditatable." We knew it was not an actual word but rather a statement on my operating system. I am not that person any longer. When I take the time to breathe, I am emptying my judgmental thoughts. Quiet and downtime also allow for more ideas to come in. Calm enables you to get out of the day-to-day spin that your thoughts keep you in. Growth happens in quiet times.

I am starting to enjoy my downtime, even if it kills me.

This might seem to be a misplaced topic, but besides my height, my previous aversion to downtime, and my not-enough-ness working against me, I also have the added reality of being Jewish.

My first brush with antisemitism

I grew up in an idyllic little town in Massachusetts without so much as a traffic light. It was also somewhat boring. We did have free reign on summer days to ride around town, hang around the town lake, and have much less scheduled lives than today's kids. I would gladly take my childhood over today's kids.

My town had a very high concentration of Jewish people, with three temples in the little town. I didn't know much about the rampant antisemitism in the world, even though there were moments when it popped into view, such as at school basketball games, when one team threw pennies on the court, which is an old trope that Jewish people are cheap. Regardless, I still felt safe in my corner of the world.

I thought towns everywhere had Jewish people who went to Hebrew schools, had Jewish holidays off from school, and went on to become bar/bat mitzvah. I was very sheltered and naive.

All this changed when I went to college.

I was at my boyfriend's fraternity party when one of the elder brothers told me why he wanted the new pledges to live in the fraternity house and not the dorms. He said, and I roughly quote, "why would I want them to live in the dorms with the 'N-----s and Jews?'" I froze. My protected world, as I knew it, changed. This was a seismic shift from my safe and secure childhood. I had heard of antisemitism of course, but it had never come this close to me.

My memory believes I said I was, in fact, Jewish, but I am blank from this point on. I learned to be a little more guarded, a little less trusting, and a lot more protective of my ethnicity. After losing 6 million of my ancestors, I believe it is necessary.

One day, I could not travel for a meeting because of an upcoming Jewish holiday, and a client who lived down South said, "I didn't know *you people* had a holiday today." Another co-worker of mine from Europe said she had found out her father was Jewish but had hidden his identity from his family because he didn't want it to impact them negatively. The rhetoric around antisemitism is staggeringly painful.

As of 2020, the world's "core" Jewish population—those identifying as Jews above all else—was estimated at 15.3 million, 0.2 percent of the 8 billion worldwide population (DellaPergola 2022). One in four Jewish Americans say they have been a target of antisemitic behavior, such as a physical attack or a racial slur, according to a 2021 report by the American Jewish Committee. These incidents happen in public, at schools, and in the workplace. "There has been a rising tide of hatred," said Andrea Lucas, a commissioner on the Equal Employment Opportunity Commission (EEOC). "Too often, instances of antisemitism in the workplace go ignored, unreported, or unaddressed."

Examples of antisemitism in the workplace include firing, not hiring, or paying someone less because the person is Jewish; assigning Jewish individuals to less-desirable work conditions; refusing to grant religious accommodations; and making anti-Jewish remarks (Hernandez, 2021). I recently heard a statistic that one in four hiring managers would not hire someone with a Jewish-sounding name. I have been associated with the talent acquisition industry for almost my whole career. Is this true? According to the research, yes. Hiring managers said in a survey that they are less likely to move forward with Jewish applicants due in part to a belief that Jews have too much "power and control"—the same antisemitic views recently espoused by Kanye West. Additionally, one in six hiring managers said leadership told them not to hire Jewish applicants, while one-third said antisemitism is common in their workplace. Just under one-third—29 percent—said antisemitism is "acceptable" at their company (Moody 2022).

In high school, I had a teacher who said using a dash in the word antisemitism made it real. Grammarly has suggested I take the hyphen out of antisemitism. The Anti-Defamation League's position is this: While removing a hyphen by itself won't defeat antisemitism, we believe this slight alteration will help to clarify understanding of this age-old hatred (Anti-Defamation League 2022).

It may seem like this discussion about being Jewish may not fit into this chapter of not measuring up, but I believe that if you are already worried about not being accepted for who and what you are, this just adds to the conundrum of not being enough. It is yet another layer that you put on to protect yourself from not measuring up. Today, there is an overwhelming amount of anti-everything. When and how does this stop perpetuating?

I have been wrestling with this over the past several years and certainly very acutely after Ahmad Aubrey was killed.

This is a piece I wrote to express my feelings:

When my son leaves the house

While my son has not lived in my house for many years, I don't fear when he leaves the house.
My son is gay, and we are Jewish, but he grew up in an area where this was largely tolerated and, to some level, accepted. When he left to go to college, he also selected a school that was very accepting on every account.
Still, I worried.
Then, he moved to other cities—Pittsburgh, San Francisco, and Los Angeles—all generally accepting cities.
But still, I worried.
Because mothers do worry.
We worry that you will make bad choices, you will drink too much, do drugs that will have deadly side effects, that you will go home with someone you shouldn't have gone home with…
I also have a beautiful daughter, but today is not the day to ramble on about how much I worry about her safety.
But trust me. I will on another day because being a woman in America has its own set of challenges.

But, for the most part, I do not worry about either of them coming home.

For the most part, I do not worry about him getting pulled over by the cops while jogging, birdwatching, driving, crossing the street, entering his home, or even being in his home, shopping, walking, talking, or getting killed in public. By.the.police.

This is unimaginable and unthinkable to me.

And every pore in my body is angry at a system that treats and has treated our black sons so ruthlessly.

I can't hug my children because they are not with me. But I know I will hug them again.

Many black mothers will never hug their sons again. And for this, I am desperately worried.

I worry that I am not doing enough and that the initial flames of outrage will burn out too quickly.

And frankly, this worries me most of all.

I am continuing my education by reading, talking to people, and having uncomfortable conversations. I know I have much to learn.

It is essential to understand and acknowledge how you came to be you. Our upbringings shape us; our physical body shapes up, and our religion shapes and identifies us. We don't have the power to change our past, but we can become more self-aware, more accepting of who we are, and then shift our mindset to envision and create the future we desire.

We always have the power to become the person we aspire to be.

CHAPTER 6

THE BUSINESS OF PEOPLE

"Take care of your employees, and they will take care
of your business. As simple as that."

—RICHARD BRANSON (2021)

I grew up in the age of talent acquisition. This is a fancy term
for hiring. I don't really care for industry jargon; please tell
me what you mean.

The new terms are complicated versions of the simpler
terms we used to use. Case in point, when and why did
the word cadence replace the words schedule, timeline, or
rhythm? When did the word journey replace the word progress? I am a word person at heart, and these "new and improved" words sound pretentious to me.

Having worked through two recessions, with a third one
looming, I have been around the employment block, but I
have never seen an employment marketplace quite like what
we are seeing right now. It is likely the greatest sociological
experiment we have ever seen.

What will happen with hybrid workers? Will Jamie Di-
mon, CEO of JP Morgan Chase, win his argument that
all employees should work in the office (Shevlin 2022)? Or,
will Meta win, allowing for remote work across the board

(Duffy 2022)? What happens to office space? Will this just be a pendulum swing, and in five years become business as pre-COVID-19 usual? I think this is likely, and we already see shades of this. But workers clearly want more choices. They have had more time with their families and less time commuting, and they don't want to give this up.

Will this help in hiring diverse candidates? I certainly hope so. Will it even out wage disparities? I hope the answer is yes. Candidates from lower-cost areas of the country can now be considered for roles in higher cost-of-living areas without having to move and pay exorbitant rent. The average rent in Manhattan rose to $5,058 in June 2022 (Frank 2022). Compensation can be based on job contribution. If you live in an expensive area such as Silicon Valley and work in an office, a cost-of-living adjustment on top of the base salary may still be necessary. But this would not be necessary for remote workers doing the same job.

My career began at a recruitment advertising agency in Boston. The agency started as a travel advertising agency, but soon clients began asking if the agency could also help create help-wanted advertisements. And with that, a new agency was born, the Haughey Group. I was a summer intern cutting tear sheets, which are print publication clippings to prove that the ad you purchased ran, and proofing ad copy. After graduation from college, I worked full-time as an account coordinator, taking ad copy over the phone for help wanted ads. This was before fax machines, computers, and the internet. This was also before the terms human resources or talent acquisition were born. We worked with the very glamorous personnel departments, usually located in the farthest reaches of company buildings. In other words, human resources and hiring departments were not considered nearly as important as they are today.

This career suited me. I liked helping clients hire people. I liked the creativity of an ad agency, and I intrinsically knew I was helping a company grow by helping them hire. It was never about an ad in the newspaper for me. I stayed in this industry until the end of my career. I saw sweeping changes led by the advent of the internet. My agency was acquired with about twenty other advertising agencies across the globe in the '90s. Another agency that was acquired at the same time was MonsterBoard. Monster revolutionized the way companies recruited talent via the internet. I loved being part of this digital revolution.

We have an obligation to make the hiring process as fair and equitable as possible. The "human capital industry" talks about employment branding, talent attraction and management, candidate engagement, retention, turnover, cost per application, and so on. So many terms, tools, and still so much room for improvement. Please tell me why companies ghost candidates, why it is necessary to have eight interviews before deciding on a candidate, and why companies pay people more when they are about to walk out the door? We are talking about people's lives.

Much is being written about the great resignation, the great realignment, the great regret, quiet quitting, and recently quiet hiring. Just for kicks, I just did a Google search on the term great resignation. Here are the results: about 365,000,000 results (0.65 seconds) (Google 2023). Amazing, but not at all surprising to me. Everyone is talking about recession, layoffs, and the economy at large. Today's latest buzz is about ChatGPT, artificial intelligence (AI) that answers questions and writes in a conversational style. Much like we talk about robots taking over for humans, ChatGPT may take over jobs such as customer service, data entry, and content creators, another name for writers (2023).

Technology will continue to evolve. We will have a slew of new terms. But until we are all replaced with AI and robots, we need to continue leading our teams. I like this quote:

> "To some, the pandemic exposed how much work had become like adult daycare. Everyone is expected to be in at a certain time. They're expected to stay till a certain time. And it's best to look busy in between."
>
> —RUSS HILL, *THE GREAT RESIGNATION: WHY MILLIONS ARE LEAVING THEIR JOBS AND WHO WILL WIN THE BATTLE FOR TALENT* (HILL 2021)

There is no greater area to focus on than our jobs as leaders to recruit, develop, retain, and even exit our employees. Frontline workers are employees within essential industries (2020) who must physically show up to their jobs and make the least amount of money in any industry. Hospitality, customer service, health care, teachers, and retail deal directly with our children, clients, and customers. Nothing highlighted this gap quite like COVID-19, where these workers put themselves in harm's way so we could eat, learn, get healthy, get sick, and buy stuff.

The research to support the problems that frontline workers experienced during COVID-19 and after COVID-19 are well documented: Frontline workers report lower job security, lower health and mental well-being, and a much higher risk of contagion. Frontline workers were more likely than teleworkers to feel that their job was insecure—12 percent versus

7 percent—and to report bad general health—6 percent versus 4 percent. They also reported lower levels of mental well-being—55 percent versus 53 percent. This was measured using the WHO-5 mental well-being scale—zero to one hundred, with people with a score below fifty considered at risk of depression—based on the frequency of positive feelings over the previous two weeks (Eurofound, 2021[6]) (Scarpetta, Carcillo, Salvatori 2022).

But things have yet to really improve post-COVID-19. One out of every five workers in the United States is employed in the retail and hospitality sector. That's more than 30 million workers. So, this isn't just a retail, restaurant, and hospitality problem; it's also an American problem. If we look at these workers' likelihood to leave this sector, their "quit rate," as the government data calls it, is almost twice as high as the national average in other sectors. This is a massive group who is leaving their jobs much more often than employees in any other sector. They also report an almost 30 percent higher likelihood to leave their jobs than we've seen in other sectors. This certainly has massive implications for the overall US economy (Fuller 2022). From talking to leaders in retail, restaurants, and hospitality, we also know there's a linkage to bottom-line performance and the customer experience. Any way you look at it, it's a pretty massive problem (Briedis 2020).

My father died toward the end of the pandemic, not from COVID-19, but from pancreatic cancer. It is a swift killer, but we tried to make the last days of his life as comfortable as possible. This would not have been possible without the help of our home care agency, Excellus. When my father came home from the hospital, he needed twenty-four-hour care. I hired Excellus after interviewing several other agencies. I immediately clicked with the owner. The first night at home was brutal because the aide didn't quite hit it off with my dad's partner's family. Everyone was scared about how and what would happen next.

Karen, the owner, was a lifesaver, and she soon found another aide and solution. Next, my dad came down with COVID-19, as did his partner, and the care became even more complex. Some aides did not want to work with COVID-19 patients, which was totally understandable. We had to change the care plan again. On top of COVID-19, a not-so-easy living situation, we also had to contend with not one, but two nor'easters. A nor'easter is a specific type of storm that moves up the East Coast and is famous for producing rain, snow, sleet, and of course, strong northeasterly winds (2015). But Karen and her aides managed every challenge and provided excellent care throughout it all.

I would often talk to the aides. They respected and were very loyal to Karen. These are frontline workers who are doing God's work, taking care of patients and their families during what is possibly the most emotional part of life, death. And she had zero turnover—zero.

One of the aides said to me, "I trust Karen. She has our backs and pays fairly. Karen always makes time to listen to us. She has also done our job, and her understanding and empathy are helpful because we all have days when we just need to vent."

More of these types of Karens, please.

I hope my point is clear here; if you take care of your employees by recognizing their accomplishments, strengths, and weaknesses, and pay them fairly for their work, you will keep them as Karen has done. You may still have turnover, but you will see far less of it. As a leader, it is your job to ensure the people who deal with your customers are taken care of; if we take good care of them, they take great care of our customers. I believe in this approach with every fiber of my being.

I took my job very seriously from a very young age—whether as a waitress, retail clerk, or a new advertising account coordinator. Early in, late out, and all the other stuff you believe will get you ahead in the world. These early work experiences have shaped me more than I realized. I had terrific mentors and learned how I wanted to lead and how I did not.

In my time as a manager, I have hired people who have ended up being top performers, fired people who I didn't want to fire, fired people who deserved to be fired, and developed people who I, frankly, sometimes, did not want to develop. I have made many mistakes, sometimes bringing my own biases into the process. But every situation is an opportunity to learn.

I hired a woman I liked in New York City because she was from a similar background. We knew some of the same people, and I liked her vibe. She turned out to be a mediocre hire—too slow to do the work and not intuitive enough to sense when something was wrong with the client. Those skills are hard to teach, but I realized I had some hiring biases. We all have them. Training for unconscious bias should be required for all people involved in hiring and managing. Unconscious biases are social stereotypes about certain groups of people that individuals form outside their own conscious awareness. Everyone holds unconscious beliefs about various social and identity groups. These biases stem from one's tendency to organize social worlds by categorizing (Navarro, 2015).

I have had to fire colleagues who I was very close to. Several sensed it was coming, and I could do nothing to give a heads-up because that is against HR protocol. One employee on our one-on-one call said, "I think I am about to be let go from the company."

I thought deeply about what I could possibly say that would not break the company code but also provide some information to someone who I liked and trusted very much.

I said, "There is nothing I can say to make you feel better right now."

I am sure this was not HR-approved, but I wanted to signal in any way I could. I had lost a close friend at the company who was let go and thought I owed it to her to give her a heads-up. I was told by HR that I could not do this, and I did not give her a heads-up. I still wrestle with this decision, and to this day, despite some reach outs on my part, she will not forgive or speak to me.

I am a company person. I towed the company line. I voiced my opinion if it was possible, but ultimately, I knew some decisions were above me. Potentially, we are doing people favors by exiting them. Not always, of course, but by and large, people tend to move on. I will not minimize that some of the exits I had to do left me feeling pretty awful. The silver lining is that they all ended up on their feet and, many, in better spots.

For employees who may be out of the new hire range but are underperforming, I believe we should try to ensure we give them the tools they need to be successful. Can they improve with the proper support? Some companies may use a stack ranking tool where you rank your employees on current performance and future potential. I know there are loads of tools, but this one works for me, and it is simple to use. It also keeps the manager accountable for their teams. What is your role if you have a "C" underperforming player? Will you put this person on a performance improvement plan (PIP), move to a different position, or exit? We owe our staff this level of rigor and commitment.

I hired a woman I did not want to hire, but my team was hell-bent on her. I sat through her presentation to the team, and I was a no-vote, but I let the team make the hiring decision. She was brilliant and filled with great ideas and even better experience. Still, her standards were extremely high, and she needed help working with anyone who didn't meet these standards, including the leaders of the company. She was not a good fit for the culture. I fired her reasonably early on, although I personally loved working with her. She made me smarter. But she could not work with her teammates, which would not fly. Was this the right decision? Could I have insisted that the team make this work? I don't think that ever quite works out once you lose the trust and confidence of your teammates and slam them repeatedly, it is likely not a fixable situation.

I coached a client who was promoted to a partner at his law firm. This wonderfully quirky, slightly older gentleman was not well suited for the traditional partnership role, which required new business development and increased billable hours. Bill is a technology genius, and is extremely analytical and detail oriented as you might expect. Everyone knew this was not a great fit. Of course, the intentions of the firm were noble, but you do have to consider the person and the goals of the company. Are they aligned? This was a classic example of trying to put a square peg into a round hole. He eventually started his own practice where he could work at his own pace in his own time. Interestingly, he was always worried about his retirement and his money situation because he has a special needs adult child. I hear about none of this when we do our check-in calls. He seems happy and totally at ease.

I fired a gentleman who was a poor sales performer. Ultimately, I had to let him go because he used the company credit card for a dating app. We had clear rules about the personal usage of corporate credit cards. He left without a blip on the radar screen. Some exits are easy, and some are difficult. Some hires are worth spending the development time on, and some are not. Our job as leaders is to make the correct determination.

I am not sure there is another industry that has as many shiny new objects as the human capital/talent acquisition marketplace. The new tools help companies become more efficient—chatbots, AI tools, video interviewing and screening, programmatic media advertising that automates and optimizes your media spend in real-time, enhanced websites that serve up only relevant candidate information, branding that delivers the messaging of what this company will be like to work for, review sites where candidates can find out in advance interview questions, salary ranges and, most importantly, what it is like to work at the company itself. A dizzying array of options help companies and candidates improve the hiring process and overall employee engagement, but I think there is still much work to do.

Despite all the new toys, the "black hole of recruiting" is well-named. Too many interviews to make a solid hiring decision takes too much time for the candidate and company. Candidates are ghosted—and also ghost companies— or recruiters delay responses long after they have promised. Many candidates hear nothing at all.

We have a long way to go to improve the candidate experience.

Let me be clear on this, I am pro-candidate. Candidates are trying to change their lives when they apply for jobs. Recruiters and people involved in the hiring process have jobs and are doing their jobs. A fundamental imbalance is in the process. Although companies have internal structures that may work against them—too much work and not enough resources—we still need to make it easier for candidates. We must find a better, sustainable way to make the hiring process more efficient and equitable for all parties. I am also pro-employee. We cannot have a one-size-fits-all approach. Correctly balancing the needs of the business with the needs of the employee will always drive better business results.

Let's never lose sight of being human.

CHAPTER 7

TAKE THE DAY OFF!

I don't know about you, but these four words send m-e into a little bit of a tizzy.

My first thought is, how can I fill up my day? Am I supposed to get errands done, get caught up on my work and sleep, and spend more time with my kids, friends, family, or significant other? What happens if something goes awry at work, and I am not available? This feels more like catch up on your life day, not take the day off day. I want to get as much done on my day off, and, obviously, this flies in the face of the intention of a day off.

The way I grew up, and certainly the way I grew up in corporate America, I believed you weren't doing work right if you weren't exhausted by Tuesday. I wanted to avoid ending up like my dad, who owned his painting contracting business. Sometimes, he was busy, but not during economic downturns and off-season. Money was tight in our house, and as a result, I have spent much of my childhood/adult life worried about money, even when it is somewhat irrational.

My brothers and I vowed that we would not let this happen to us. Each of us picked professions that suited us. But one of the distinct differences is that they had wives to help at home. I was divorced with minimal financial support from my ex-husband. Fear of financial failure fueled me. If I wasn't busy, I wasn't worth paying. When I told people how busy and stressed I was, it validated my corporate existence. This was the only path I saw to advance my career, and it worked for quite a while.

Vacations?

My best friend got married in Perugia at a castle in Italy during the Amanda Knox trial. I was interviewing candidates in my hotel room while looking at the beauty of Umbria. On a girls' trip in Arizona, I had to sneak a phone call in the bushes outside of the spa and the no-call zone. In Nashville, I was hanging out a car window working on a retainer agreement in transit. In Napa, I stepped out of a wine tasting class to find out about a client issue. My entire family goes on an annual trip around Christmas time, and I was never not chasing a year-end contract signature.

None of this is surprising if you look at the research: American workers are notorious for being workaholics. Since March 2020, an overwhelming majority of US employees have shortened, postponed, or canceled their vacation time. Another recent study found that 26 percent of respondents had never taken two weeks of vacation at one time. And the Center for Economic and Policy Research has gone so far as to call the US the "No Vacation Nation." (2020). On average, employees in the US take fourteen days off per year, while workers in European countries like Spain, France, Germany, and even the UK take twenty-four days, according to workforce tech solutions company Skynova (May 2019).

Going on holiday makes you feel more present and stimulated. "When we travel, we are usually breaking our normal routine," says Richard Davidson, professor of psychology and psychiatry at the University of Wisconsin-Madison and founder of the Center for Healthy Minds (2022). That means we can't operate on autopilot. This study followed more than twelve thousand middle-aged men at high risk for heart disease. In the end, those who took more yearly vacations were less likely to die from any cause, including heart attacks and other cardiovascular problems (2021).

Stress raises levels of certain hormones, such as cortisol and adrenaline. In the short term, this can be helpful, triggering the "fight or flight" response that helps you deal with immediate threats. But over time, chronic stress can increase your risk for health issues, including heart disease. A study released by the American Psychological Association concluded that time off helps to reduce stress by removing people from the activities and environments that they associate with anxiety (2018). Taking time off improves the capacity to learn. When your brain is completely relaxed, it consolidates knowledge and brainpower. "Neuroscience is so clear, through PET scans and MRIs, that the 'aha' moment comes when you're in a relaxed state of mind," says Brigid Schulte, author of *Overwhelmed: Work, Love and Play When No One Has the Time*. That's why you have your best ideas on a walk, in the shower, or on vacation (2000).

Vacation time improves sleep.

Restless nights are a common complaint—one of my issues—often stemming from the fact that we have too much on our minds. Researchers say time off from work can help interrupt the habits that disrupt sleep, like working late into the night or checking your cell phone before bed. Another reason your sleep improves while on holiday and extends after your return is that a new bed helps you dissociate from your negative sleep patterns back home.

A study conducted by New Zealand Air asked participants on vacation to wear a wrist device that would monitor their quality of sleep starting three days before their holiday until three days after their return.

They also kept a sleep diary, and were measured for reaction times before, during, and after their trip. Researchers found that after two to three days of vacation, the participants averaged an hour more of good-quality sleep and experienced an 80 percent improvement in their reaction times. When they returned home, they slept close to an hour more, and their reaction time was 30 to 40 percent higher than before the trip (2017).

The Hustle

Another stalwart part of American corporate culture is the hustle, which in my mind, glorifies workaholism. I have always lived in the hustle—always. As far back as I can remember, I was always moving. I talked fast and moved faster, or vice versa, depending on the day. I don't know if this was a function of trying to stay up to par with my older brothers, but nevertheless, it is how I used to operate. I had one manager, who I disliked intensely, who called me the "Tasmanian Devil." One client I had down South used to ask me to speak slower in my presentations. Before I met another client for the first time, she said she knew I was going to be a smaller person based on how fast I moved.

You don't realize how hustle and comparison infiltrate your life. Hustle is what makes a winner. "She is hustling, she is a go-getter." Hustle is a very valued commodity in our corporate lives. You often hear about a side hustle if you need to make more than what you are making in your full-time job. Hustle. Hustle. Hustle. If you are in sales, you must have x number of calls/appointments to convert to x number of sales. And look how well Suzy Sunshine is doing this quarter. Shoot, I must be a horrible salesperson. And your leaders are looking at these numbers constantly. As with any other gig you reside in, there are ways you are evaluated that keep you in the hustle. But clearly, something must change given the nature of our current workforce.

If you are paying attention, this COVID-19 era has been marked by new terms, "the Great Resignation" being the leading term for employees quitting to find greener and more pleasant pastures. We are now reading about the regret many employees have about leaving and finding new jobs during the COVID-19 years. But let's not get tangled up in terminology here because many left for tangible reasons.

According to a study by Deloitte, 77 percent of people have experienced burnout at their job, and 42 percent have left their jobs because they felt burned out. This results from mental and emotional stress due to working long hours and trying to keep up with unrealistic expectations set by the toxic excesses of hustle culture. Add in working from home and COVID-19, and you have a cauldron of ways to burn people at the stake, specifically, women. More than half of the five thousand women surveyed across ten countries said they plan to leave their current employer within two years. Additionally, 10 percent were currently looking for a new job with another organization—four percentage points more than in 2021. **Endless hustling doesn't benefit any-one.** Employees grow dissatisfied and unproductive, while employers pay for it. It's been calculated that burned-out and otherwise disengaged employees cost companies as much as 34 percent of their annual salaries (2022).

Hands down, coaching is the best job I have ever had. The career fulfillment is like nothing I have ever experienced before. Being able to help people become the best version of themselves is humbling and deeply existentially rewarding. My thirst for knowledge and endless curiosity has led me down so many interesting paths. I am fascinated with how the mind works. How and why do we make the decisions we make? What can we do differently to change our outcomes? Fear largely runs our lives in ways we don't even realize. It rules our decision making if we let it.

My mindset coach, Tracy Litt, taught me more than any other person or teacher ever has. We can manage our thoughts instead of letting our thoughts—roughly sixty thousand per day—rule us (2022). Of these thoughts, about 80 percent are negative thoughts (2022). I did not know I didn't have to believe or follow my thoughts. I thought they were running the show. Surely, they knew what they were doing and had my best interests at heart. No, not really.

Do you mean beating myself up, a condition I was very used to, was optional? I was comfortable letting my thoughts make my decisions—never letting myself get too high or too low lest the other shoe drops. I believed this was the way to manage my attitude and performance. I was wrong.

This hustle mentality is what I took with me as I started my coaching practice. How many clients? How many sessions? How to set up a cost structure? And on and on. My new measurement is to evaluate how my clients are doing first. Do they see a change in themselves? Are they reaching the goals they set up for coaching? Of course, I still measure myself on a business scale because I want to serve more people and create a thriving business, which I have.

One day, I was in a session with my coach, and she said, "Donna, you are doing great. Probably better than 90 percent of the newer coaches out there. You should be so proud!"

I shrugged my shoulders and said, "Yeah."

Obviously, I didn't convince her at all that I was, in fact, proud of myself.

She said, "You have new clients, clients that renew, a high rate of referrals, and have created several group programs! What is going on with you?" Then she said, "Are you waiting for the other shoe to drop?"

I said, "Yes."

This is how I had been conditioned.

Don't get too high because you never know when the other shoe will drop. Inevitably, it did in my corporate life— win a client today, lose a client tomorrow.

Balancing the highs and lows was essential for me to manage my emotions.

She rushed right at me and said, "*You* are the fucking shoe!" I have this on video.

Huh, lightbulb moment for me. "I am the fucking shoe." And, so are you.

I can decide how I respond to any given situation. I can be happy, support myself with the wins, and be gentler on myself for the losses, or as I like to call them now, the learning moments.

This conversation changed my life.

Now, when I have a less-than-stellar moment, I don't stress about it as much. I really don't because I am the fucking shoe.

More pearls of wisdom from my coach:

"Nothing means anything until you give it meaning."

Sounds like a simple phrase, but it is actually the opposite.

We spend so much time placing meaning on things, people, and situations without all the facts.

Many times after I relayed to her that I was sure I knew what was going on because I knew the person and had history that told me what the outcome would be, she would simply say, "You actually don't know."

And she was right.

We have zero chance of changing a situation or ourselves if we live in our own assumptions and stories.

Levity is another nugget that was foreign to me in my corporate life. Being serious about our work doesn't mean you have to take yourself so seriously. My coach started many of our group sessions with dancing and singing. It loosened us all up.

The following is an interesting article excerpt about why levity is important in our corporate and everyday life.

Here are just three reasons it pays to lighten up:

- **More memorable communication:** Whether you're about to make a presentation to senior management to get funding for your big idea, pitch a sales prospect who could make your year, or try to engage a troop of distracted campfire girls, great communicators know that a bit of humor goes a long way toward making you and your messages more memorable. One caveat is you have to know your audience; humor won't work in every situation—trust me on this.

- **Bigger, better ideas:** The work world isn't suffering from a dearth of tedious, go-nowhere, stiff, brainstorming sessions. Research shows you can boost scores on standardized tests of creativity by exposing people to humor or other conditions that establish a playful atmosphere.
- **A more successful you:** Leaders who use more levity experience higher employee productivity, engagement, and retention. For individuals, the financial rewards hit even closer to home: people with a sense of humor climb the corporate ladder more quickly and earn more money than their peers. Quite simply, executives hire and promote the humorous more often than the dour. Wouldn't you (2023)?

My mission in life is to stop glorifying work over everything else. Work does not define you.

Working hard is *not* the leading metric for success—not by a long shot. Success and ease can and do go hand in hand. Ease allows space and thinking time and improved decision-making. Stress limits your ability to think more broadly.

Although it almost feels irresponsible when running your own business, or as a working professional, mother, and so on to take the day off, it is precisely the opposite. It is essential for growth, self-care, and, most importantly, your sanity.

Take the damn day off because you need it; you will be a better employee, parent, partner, and human. Take the day off to model great behavior for the people around you. Stop worrying about what other people think because you don't know what they are thinking.

So, if it has been a while, *take or schedule a day off and enjoy yourself! Have some fun!*

And I will do the same after this book is published.

CHAPTER 8

THE CURSE OF THE DREADED FITTED SHEET

Is there anything more frustrating than trying to get a fitted sheet on a bed? Three corners work, and then the fourth is like a sumo-wrestling match. A task that should be easy and take minimal time causes me to sweat yet is not listed in my Fit Tracker for an exercise option. It should be! Sometimes, this is embarrassing because I don't even have the sheet lined up correctly. Then, when it is in the correct direction, that fourth corner fit always lurks in the back of my mind. "Will it work this time?" And don't even get me started on Marie Kondo. No, folding and changing sheets does not spark joy in me. As of this writing and the birth of her third child, I am not sure it sparks much joy in Marie either.

Like all things that require effort, I have become adept at fourth corner fitting techniques. When I wrote the beginning of this chapter, I was having some communication challenges with a close family member. How could I make our relationship and style of communication work better? This inner dialogue with myself may be a good metaphor for life and relationships with others.

There are always relationships fraught with the fourth corner. When you are just not sure how to navigate the fit properly, you are walking on eggshells, wondering what to say/do/not do. You learn survival techniques to ensure the relationship stays at a peaceful equilibrium. We all do it. But at what cost to ourselves?

Maybe some answers lie in the sheet metaphor:

- If the last corner doesn't fit, loosen the other three corners.
    - In other words, be ready to loosen up.
    - Relationships need give and take.
- Sometimes relationships, like sheets, need more ease.
    - Don't be so stuck in your approach that you can't try a different way to look at things.
    - Being gentler and more open might bring more favorable results.
    - Someone else might have a better solution.
- Give it a rest—pun intended.
    - Walking away and coming back later sometimes helps and gives some much-needed perspective.
    - I wish I had leveraged this approach more often. Leaving a conversation that is not going well and taking a little hiatus can save so many headaches. When you are saying things in the heat of anger and having to backtrack about what you said, you often lose sight of the original issue.
- Know when to fold 'em.
    - Sometimes you just gotta buy new sheets and start over.
    - Agreeing to disagree saves so much time and energy. Once you agree to this, hopefully you can move on.
- Changing sheets and relationships are lifelong, regular exercises.

- If you care enough, you have time to get it right.
- Give yourself and the other person some grace.
- When we get stuck in being right, nobody wins. And we shut ourselves off from greater communication.
- If your job, relationship, and kids are important to you, and you care deeply, give others some room to disagree with you or share different perspectives. Being right can be lonely and overrated.
- *No one* is perfect.

I have spoken to hundreds of people about their war stories at work. Some stories are so head-scratchingly horrible that you wonder how people have and stay in their jobs. Every company has one, two, or more employees, and you wonder how they (1) are still there, and (2) ever got promoted. I don't want to say that it is usually a middle-aged white man, but if the shoe fits.

We all have blind spots. We are human. Sometimes these blind spots don't allow seeing the people working for us in the correct light. This has happened to me before. I had one employee I absolutely adored. I thought she would be great to work on another very large account requiring a move to another city. She was not. But I still had to take time to process that she was not a fit. She was a great employee, but this was not the right place for her. We had to move her back to her original market on a new team.

She was the fourth corner. Our job as leaders is to put our employees in the right roles. Sometimes, an underperforming employee is just not in the correct position. Not all people work in all situations, which seems obvious when you hear it, but we don't always act on it.

Here is another pet peeve of mine. Before transitioning an employee who knows the culture out of the company, try seeing if there is a better fit someplace else in the company. This simple act shows other employees that the company is committed to finding and placing the right talent in the right place. It won't work for everyone, but it is worth the effort.

I am trained as a core energy coach. We coach the person and not the situation.

Core Energy Coaching™ is a methodology focused on getting to the root—or "core"—of an individual's challenges by identifying and shifting inner thoughts, beliefs, and emotions that block a client's success. We all have seven energy levels that we rotate through at any given time, but we do have dominant levels. None of the levels are necessarily good or bad, but it does provide us with information about where your head is at.

Here is how iPEC, my coach training program, quickly defines energy, energy levels, and how understanding energy can impact your relationships (iPEC 2023).

When you gain a deeper understanding of the different types of energy, suddenly, people's "unexpected" responses will make more sense, and you'll be in a better position to engage from a more informed place (2018).

- **Level 1:** Feeling lost. Stuck. Lack of choice. I can't. I have to. Fearful.
- **Level 2:** Anger. Combativeness. Resisting or fighting energy.
- **Level 3:** Rationalizing. Fine. Coping.
- **Level 4:** Care. Compassion. Service to others.
- **Level 5:** Reconciliation. Win-win. Solution-focused.
- **Level 6:** Intuition. Creative genius. Visionary.
- **Level 7:** Absolute Passion. Non-judgment. Oneness.

Through learning more about energy, you'll have a framework and understand not only what's going on energetically with the people on your team, but with *yourself* as well.

This new level of insight will help you connect more meaningfully with coworkers, employees, patients, prospects, or clients. You'll also be able to identify personal emotions or triggers that may interfere with a clear, neutral understanding of a situation. As a result, you'll be better equipped to deliver an effective, compassionate response and lead your team to better performance (2021).

I assess my clients, as well as my own life, through this energy lens. I want to focus on how these levels manifest in the workplace and their lives outside work. We often look at situations with a singular outcome, but understanding where someone's energy level is helps us create a plan for a desired result. If someone is at level 1 and in victim/poor me/I lose mode, getting them to a win/win level 5 is too big of a leap. I encourage you to read *Energy Leadership* by the founder of iPEC, Bruce Schneider. It will give you a much deeper overview of the energy levels.

I had one manager reporting to me who looked at situations much differently than I did. I would say he operated at level 2 energy—win/lose, us against them. I believe I operated at more of a level 4 except when it related to him. He triggered me all over the place. We rarely, if ever, saw eye to eye. I realized I was stuck on being right and not on what the best outcome of the situation was. Today, if I coach someone in a win/lose mindset, I let them vent. I acknowledge their feelings and validate that it is normal to feel like they do.

Here is a perfect example of how I think coach training would benefit corporate America. I didn't see much of an effort to solve difficult employee relationships other than to chalk it up to personality differences. Or, to say figure it out and move on. Imagine a world where we try to repair, understand, and improve relationship dynamics.

If another department delivered shoddy work or delivered it late, or both, clearly it makes perfect sense that you would be disappointed. But, instead of angrily pointing out the obvious underperformance, how can we achieve our desired outcome? An angry email or phone call—what is that?—or email to a superior that feels all too common in corporate generally does not solve the problem.

If I am coaching this person, I may ask, "What is another way we can view this situation?" "What else might be going on here?" "What is the best possible outcome?"

Of course, it is frustrating that you wanted the work sooner and the work missed the mark, but how can we move forward? The blame game doesn't get us to the next step. I wish every corporate human who ever walked the face of the earth would understand this. Read it, print it out on their computer, make it a screen saver, and have signage all over the place.

Winning is overrated

One of my clients, who is one of the finest humans I know, was working with a new chief marketing officer who routinely threw my client's teams under the bus, and used numbers that she could not back up in her presentations. We spent a lot of time talking about her, and she was the definition of toxic. We mentioned this relationship to the CEO and CRO on our coaching status check-in call. They did not take the bait. My client could not find common ground with this person, which is almost unheard of. No surprise, my client eventually called me to tell me the big news that the CMO would be exited from the company. The CEO told my client she had thrown another team under the bus in a meeting, which was the last straw. It reflected poorly on the team and the company to have a non-team player. Kudos to the CEO and CRO for not gossiping or backstabbing this person, rather they just took action.

I wish more companies would take action on toxic employees. I know there would be a lot less turnover in companies if employees saw companies act against toxic employees. It is disheartening and demotivating, to say the least, to see this behavior tolerated and, many times, rewarded.

If I was coaching the now-departed employee, we might have dug into her need to be right and why she needed to elevate her team at the expense of others. Sometimes, people are not aware of their behavior and don't realize their actions make them look the exact opposite of what they are trying to accomplish.

Awareness is the first step to making changes. My client stayed calm and patient with herself. Coaching helped her realize this wasn't about her and her teams. Since I have been around the block a few times, I knew it was likely this person would flame out. Another benefit of coaching is to help see a situation from different perspectives. I understand it is hard to see the whole playing field when you are deep in the heart of a sticky situation.

A dear friend and colleague I interviewed for this book section said she had a boss who used to start her calls with, "Let me tell you how I am going to ride your ass this week, Deb." How is that for a beginning of a call? It fills you with respect and support for your manager, right? When my friend corrected her boss and said, "My name is not Deb. It is Debbie." Her boss said, "There are too many Debbie's around here, so to me, you are Deb." Um, outstanding leadership. I think not. Good leaders build their teams up; they do not tear them down. Next boss, please.

Toxic cultures have a tremendous bottom-line impact:

One in five Americans has left a job in the past five years due to bad company culture. The cost of that turnover is an estimated $223 billion, according to a new SHRM report on workplace culture. "Billions of wasted dollars. Millions of miserable people. It's not a warzone—it's the state of the American workplace," said SHRM President and CEO Johnny C. Taylor, Jr., SHRM-SCP.

"Toxicity itself isn't new. But now that we know the high costs and how managers can improve workplaces, there's no excuse for inaction."

The report, "The High Cost of a Toxic Workplace Culture," surveyed American workers to explore the impact of workplace culture on both the well-being of workers and the bottom line of businesses. It found toxic culture costs companies a fortune in turnover and absenteeism; highlighted common indicators of bad workplace cultures, such as discrimination and harassment; and underscored the alarming impacts on employees. The research also uncovered a seemingly critical skills gap at the management level. SHRM found employees hold managers—more than leadership or HR—most responsible for culture. They also say their managers often lack the soft skills needed to effectively listen, communicate, and ultimately lead (SHRM 2019).

The "great resignation" is the opposite of fine. People were fed up; nothing and no one was fine. Employees were cooped up in their homes, many with kids in tow, working and living all at the same time with little to no breaks in between. Companies were not keeping up with employee needs because some employees were in the office, some were out, the economy was nuts, and they may not have had the training to manage such a highly complex situation as COVID-19, post-COVID-19, an erratic economy, hybrid, remote work, and rising employee unease. And the dam broke.

I hope by the time this book is in print, companies will have figured out a better way to manage employee engagement. But, if I am being frank, I think it is going to take a lot more time. COVID-19 has obviously changed the way companies manage. Before COVID-19, many companies would not think of a remote or hybrid workforce. Today, it has certainly been proven that work, and in fact, good work, was done when employees were at home. I consulted at a company in South Carolina where we were trying to cut operating expenses. I said to the CEO that we should eliminate the office space. He was adamant that his team needed to work together to be the most productive. The world shut down a month later, and he is no longer the CEO.

Companies want to see their employees in person. They want to see in-person collaboration, water cooler chats, unscheduled conversations, and it is simply easier to get a pulse on employees while they are in the office. Although I believe Zoom, Slack, Teams, and all the other great tools have enabled businesses to keep running, they do not replace in-person collaboration, so I completely understand why companies want to see more employees back in the office. The next few years will be very telling. I hope hybrid is here to stay and employees don't have to give up so much of their personal lives to succeed at companies.

Outside of work, I have also had personal relationships that were award-winning eggshell walking exercises. We all have different relationships in our lives, and they all serve different purposes. But if you have relationships where you are uncomfortable being yourself or sacrifice your time and energy to please someone else, you may have a fourth corner relationship situation.

Do we need to ditch those relationships as soon as possible? No, not necessarily. This is an opportunity for you to speak up for yourself and define new boundaries and limits. Dealing with these types of relationships differently will help grow you in ways that easier relationships do not.

If you have driven the kids after school but realize it is a significant drain on your schedule, you can simply ask to take turns driving. If you have never done this before, it will feel like a significant change to you, and may even be hard to get the words out of your mouth. Once you say it out loud, you may find yourself asking, "why didn't I just do this sooner?"

Our friends, partners, and co-workers are not mind readers. If we are dissatisfied with the way our relationship stands, within reason, we have the power to change the dynamics.

You have the power to manage the curse of the fourth corner of a dreaded fitted sheet.

CHAPTER 9

ROME WASN'T BUILT IN A DAY

This quote helps me to be more patient with myself. In case you are interested, it took 1,229 years to build Rome, counting from its founding until its collapse (Discovery 2020). Surely, it would take me less time to clean out my house of twenty-six years.

I had to start somewhere, so I decided to wade through the thousands of pictures I had yet to organize. Oh, some of the hairstyles and outfits made me cringe. In one picture, I literally looked like an elf. Who let me leave the house looking like that? I relived so many moments in my life through this experience—my high school years; seeing my mother alive and vibrant; my college years; my family and friends, many who are still by my side; my children; and my relationships.

I began to look at this move as a gift—a time to reflect on my life and see how fortunate I have been. I wasn't cleaning out my house because of a death or a financial issue. I chose to move out and capitalize on the hot real estate market during COVID-19.

Next, I tackled the basement. Cleaning out a musty packed basement—is there any other kind?—full of stuff was overwhelming. I mean, who knew how prolific my kids' art skills were? How many poems had they written? How much pottery had they created? How many cards had they written? Apparently, I am an incredible mother!

It was extremely difficult to decide what to keep and what to throw away. But I did it by taking baby steps. I went box by box and room by room. It was helpful to break down this large, overwhelming task into bite-size pieces. I created piles for keeping, possibly keeping, and getting rid of. This project became much more manageable when I put this system in place.

I set up time and space to spread out and go through several boxes at a time. I put things I was never going to use again that still had some life left in them for sale on Facebook Marketplace; I donated other things and gave away other items that would be useful in another home. By the end of this process, I felt lighter. I was proud of myself. I was ready to start fresh in my new life.

Research supports the baby-step approach.

"This may be the simplest yet the most effective strategy we can use, as consistency and learning to build on small wins are the keys to success. The happiest and most successful people will tell you that they have achieved their life and work success by taking small steps and making one positive choice after another" (Scuderi 2013).

Look for the small victories

Building a solid career, and life is like cleaning out your house. A small victory is realistic and achievable. This goal will vary depending on what you are trying to accomplish, but no matter what, dividing a larger task into smaller ones will help keep you motivated. It was a huge sense of accomplishment as I completed each room, and it encouraged me to move on to the next room and the next.

Many of us want career success, but let's first define what career success means to you.

What do you want to accomplish in your career? I generally don't use the question, "Where do you want to be in five years?" None of us really knows the answer to this question. Life can change in a minute. What are your intentions? Intentions are expansive to me, and goals are limiting. If I lose eight pounds instead of ten, have I failed? But if my intention was to lose weight and not a specific number, I can feel progress along the way. Careers are like this—progress along the way.

If you want career success, then you must realize it will take time.

Here are some tips.

- Take a course or certificate program in an area you are interested in.
    - Some companies offer free courses on their intranet.
    - I have taken free courses via Coursera.
    - Sometimes your company may have a professional development budget for this purpose. Ask your HR person or manager.
- Take a course that may help you with your next career move.
    - Need to get better at Excel, forecasting, or programming? Take a course.
    - This may require that you meet with your manager to see what will be necessary for your next role, or

you can read the job description for positions you are interested in and see what your gap areas may be.
- Network at the company.
  - Who are your role models? Reach out and set up meetings to see if they would be open to mentoring or regular meet and greets.
  - Affinity groups are great for meeting like-minded people.
- Network outside of the company.
  - Meetups
  - Professional events
  - Fun events: who says you can't find your next gig having fun?
  - I am sure there are more business deals completed on golf courses than we could count.
- Leverage LinkedIn.
  - Update your profile regularly.
  - Take LinkedIn courses.
  - Join groups on LinkedIn. I think they are vastly underutilized.
  - Comment on posts you are interested in.
  - Follow people you admire and can learn from.
  - Start posting about topics that matter to you. You will gain a following and possibly even find your next job this way.
- None of this must be done all at once. Pick something that feels manageable to you.
- Remember to track your activity and progress along the way!

You will have days when you mess up at work. We all make mistakes. You may be exited or laid off, as it's happening regularly at this writing. This does not mean your career is over. I may ask you, "What is the likelihood that you will never work again?" when you start spinning about your life/work being over. You will work again. And, you will learn and grow from each experience, even though it is painful.

I researched how long it takes to make sustainable changes. "On average, it takes more than two months before a new behavior becomes automatic—sixty-six days to be exact. And how long it takes a new habit to form can vary widely depending on the behavior, the person, and the circumstances. In this research study, it took anywhere from 18 days to 254 days for people to form a new habit" (Clear).

I love this next part of the research and want to print it on a plaque or T-shirt. Many times, we believe if we mess up, then we are completely off track, but the research says otherwise:

"The researchers also found that 'missing one opportunity to perform the behavior did not materially affect the habit formation process.'" In other words, it doesn't matter if you mess up every now and then. Building better habits is not an all-or-nothing process (Clear). *Phew.* Type it. Say it out loud. Do something with this. All or nothing is not the only or best way to go.

Here is the best nugget and highest truth of all:

The only way to get to day five hundred is to start with day one.

So, forget about the number and focus on doing the work.

I had so many moments in my successful career where I had the opportunity to make changes. When my son said, "You don't spend enough time being my mom," that should have done it, right? I gave my notice multiple times. I lived on a plane. I worked late and was accessible much of the time. I dreamed of being hospitalized so I could rest. I did reduce my work week after my first notice. But I was never able to make *sustainable* changes. These changes don't start with your schedule or with your company, they start with you. I was the problem all along.

Although I worked for a caring company, most companies are not trying to identify and/or dial back workaholics. This may be pre-pandemic thinking, but I still believe companies have a long way to go to take care of their employees. Regardless of this, I was the one who had to set boundaries. I was the one who had to start believing that working through sickness was best suited for marriage, not work. Answering late-night emails and sleeping with my phone under my pillow did not make me a better employee. I needed this external validation like a plant needs water. Maybe I should have been born a cactus.

Once I started to do this inner work, fireworks went off in my body. Do you mean I am enough even if I don't beat the crap out of myself? I am enough simply because I am? Whoa. Full stop. I thought this was a load of crap when I started working with my coach. Complete BS. After all, didn't I prove how successful I had been in my corporate career with this behavior?

"Exactly," she replied. "Exactly the point."

"Huh?" I asked.

"How happy were you in your corporate career? Did you ever feel like it was good enough? That you were good enough?"

"No," I said. "Or certainly not often enough."

"Now, you get to make different choices."

I am enough just because I am.

When you adopt this belief system as your life mantra, you look at the world differently.

I am not rivaling the time it took to build Rome, but it certainly took me a long time to embrace the new, or actual, me. One of the many reasons I love coaching is because I want it to be easier for my clients than it was for me. I have been on the other side. I also know some of you reading this will debunk the theory that "it doesn't need to be so hard." Pay attention to that resistance, just like your body gives you signals that you likely ignore, as I did.

Resistance equals I still have some blocks to uncover. We all do.

I want to be as specific as possible about the word resistance. When my coach was praising me, I couldn't let that in. She must be wrong because I knew better. When you feel this need to fight back or be right or share your more knowledgeable opinion, this is resistance.

I am working with a new LinkedIn coach to improve my LinkedIn game. He is rearchitecting the way I post on LinkedIn—always with a call to action (CTA). I have prided myself on showing up, being more vulnerable, and providing some tidbits along the way, sometimes gently talking about an upcoming program or two—gently. He had me add a specific CTA on my last post. I resisted hard. The stories I told myself propagated in my head. What will people think? Is Donna just trying to sell coaching? We will stop following her and so on.

To cut to the chase here, I posted. Within one day, I had four new appointments. The resistance was my fear. The resistance was my fear of judgment.

In setting up interviews for this book, I had the usual suspects—coaches, former colleagues, and clients—but I had not yet considered my children's point of view (POV). This book is about my corporate career and the lessons I learned. Who better to help tell this story than my children? So, with this in mind, I decided to interview my twenty-five-year-old daughter.

With an open mind, ears, and heart, I conducted the interview. I asked if she had ever seen me satisfied in my career. She said she didn't remember this emotion. She did not understand the purpose of my job because it seemed to make me miserable.

Now, I understand there is a lot a child doesn't understand about work, but kids are wise, and this is how she saw me. I cannot ignore this fact. I worked hard to support my children as a single mother. But her feelings are valid, regardless of what I did, even if they may be somewhat naive at times. She went on to say that I am a far better listener today than I was then, and this has not gone unnoticed by either of my children. I am also more patient and easier to be around than I was in my previous life. I will take this as a win!

If you are reading this, you may wonder what you can personally do to make the changes you seek. Hopefully, I have made the point that change takes time. You can't just want things to change without, well, changing.

"Nothing changes if nothing changes."

Many people come to coaching wanting to make changes, so what might be something we could work on together? First, I have you fill out an in-depth intake form telling me about yourself and what you expect and want from coaching. I also add a vision statement that asks what you want to feel like after six months of coaching.

"What will you tell your close friend about how you are feeling?"

"How will you know you have changed?"

On our first session, we review this intake form.

And, toward the end of our work together, I will reflect your words back to you so you can see how far you have come.

One of my favorite parts about coaching is being able to share and participate in your progress. In my corporate life, I would call this your return on investment. Many people overlook their progress. How does this have anything to do with change? That's a good question. The answer is, "everything."

We tend to overlook all the things we do well. If something is easy for us, it must not be worth noting. This document gives us a starting point to reflect on and grow. It brings back a measure of pride to see how far you've come. And this helps you become more confident. Confidence is at the root of most of my coaching engagements. Confidence is an infinite resource, and it is always possible to become more confident.

In between sessions, you fill out a much shorter form. One of the questions I ask is this:

"Now praise yourself, tell me why you are awesome."

How often are you praising yourself in your everyday life? Start now.

My client had a less-than-stellar new employee who the CEO took a disliking to. My client worked with me to discuss possibilities for turning this situation around. She laid out clear expectations for the employee and shared some of the feedback in a very nonthreatening way. She wanted to get the point across that they were in this together, and she wanted to help.

A few sessions later, I asked how the employee was doing, and she said, "great."

I asked if she had listed this as one of her accomplishments, and she said, "no."

Hello, turning around a fledgling employee to be a solid performer is one of the most valuable tools for a manager. If we could reduce turnover and turn underperforming employees around, companies would save billions of dollars in training, hiring, recruiting, onboarding, loss of knowledge capital, and so on. But because this came naturally to her, she overlooked listing this as an area deserving of praise. Nope, put it down!

It is ingrained in our female society to be humble and to talk less about ourselves and all that rot. In my Friday sessions of my Corporate Leadership Development Program, we make each woman talk about something they are proud of for the week. So much hedging at the beginning of this, "my team did x, I didn't do as well as Susie Smith, but I did x," By the end of our six-week program, the women are exceptional at talking about themselves and what they have accomplished.

Be proud of who you are and the progress you have made.

If I can leave you with some additional sage advice, don't be the packrat I was and keep every single item ever created by your children. And, if you don't have kids, you don't have to save every keepsake—this is why we have Instagram! And beyond this, if you want to make changes in your life, you can do so. But it won't take one thousand years. It just takes time.

CHAPTER 10

I AM A RECOVERING WORKAHOLIC

As I revisit my post-corporate life, I can truthfully say I was proud of the title, workaholic. It secretly made me smile to know people thought I was working so hard. It filled me with tremendous pride, as if I was in an exclusive club.

- I slept with my phone by my side lest I let a single email go without a quick response.
- I got into the office early to start my day and worked until whenever necessary to complete whatever I needed to get to that day or for the week ahead.
- My clients and teams had twenty-four/seven access to me.
- I was driven to the point of lunacy.
- My work came first.

Even though those closest to me thought I worked too much, I really thought I managed my work/life situation pretty well. I went to important school events and after school activities, picked up and dropped off my kids, went to parent/teacher conferences, went to dance competitions galore, scheduled playdates, and all the other logistics and love that parents handle.

Although I knew not everyone worked the way I did, I also rationalized that plenty of people worked more than I did. Another difference for me is that I could not dial back the pressure I put on myself. I took everything so seriously. On the off chance that I had a quieter week, I was worried I wasn't doing enough. So, the cycle of work and worry never ended, which is not a recommended combination.

These are the stories we tell ourselves as we do the things we think we need to do to survive and thrive in our jobs, right? I still see the effects of my work-life imbalance on my daughter. I can see her body tense up when I reach to pick up a call or text even now.

One weekend, while I was still working my corporate job, she begged me not to do any work. I got an important work call on Friday afternoon and honored my daughter's wishes.

"This is our last mother/daughter weekend of my college career," she said.

On Sunday, once I was back at the airport, I emailed my boss to update her on the situation. She asked, "When did you find out about this issue?"

I replied, "Friday."

She said, "It's Sunday."

Not such a subtle code for "you should have called or alerted me sooner."

I answered, "I was with Hannah for the weekend."

No response.

So yes, I did some considerable damage to my daughter. But I also see that she has much stronger boundaries than I did. She closes her laptop at the end of her workday and is done until the next day. She has a clear distinction between work and life. Although I certainly caused some damage, I know I also showed both of my kids how not to work, a small but meaningful consolation prize.

I asked Hannah as part of my interview with her how she described me to her college friends before I met them, and without hesitation, she said, "I told them you were a psychopath... about work."

The comment hit me hard. I had horrible boundaries. Too much of my self-worth was tied to my work persona.

I wanted to investigate what research was out there for adult children of workaholics. Little did I know there is an actual term for this condition—ACOW. The University of North Carolina conducted the first study on ACOWs and found they had higher levels of depression and anxiety, and believed events outside themselves controlled their lives, compared to adults from non-workaholic homes. Their scars manifest as an outer-directed reliance on others for decision-making, and a lack of inner confidence associated with more significant anxiety and depression than in the population at large (2021).

These results match similar studies on adult children of alcoholics. In another study, my colleagues and I wanted to see if there was a difference in psychological adjustment between ACOWs and children of alcoholics. Those who reported growing up with a workaholic parent had higher depression levels and higher rates of parentification—carrying adult responsibilities when still children—than a control group of adult children from alcoholic homes (Forbes 2021).

Well, this research certainly didn't warm my heart, and to date, I don't see these effects fully on my kids, though both would describe themselves as having anxiety. Their dad had many of the traits of an alcoholic, so my children are dealing with a double whammy.

I was in Las Vegas at a conference missing my son's seventh birthday. I sat at the window in my room and cried, thinking, how is work worth missing a milestone event? When you are with your corporate crew, you all have war stories of what you have missed for the cause of corporate life.

I flew to Arkansas from Boston in a snowstorm for a two-hour meeting before flying out to Israel the next day. It is not easy to get to Bentonville, Arkansas, on a clear day, never mind a snowy day. There were no direct flights to Bentonville. We were working on a retainer pricing agreement that had to be completed. It never crossed my mind not to go on this trip. With air travel being what it is today, there is little chance I would have been able to make this happen.

The insanity didn't end here. While on my son's bar mitzvah trip in Israel with my temple and my dad, I scheduled a client meeting. I thought it was cool to go to a client meeting in a different country.

Here is the actual definition of the suffix -aholic:

> *aholic. Suffix. The definition of aholic is someone who is addicted or obsessive about something. An example of the aholic suffix is a shopaholic, someone who shops a lot.*

Harvard Business Review has done several studies on workaholics:

> … workaholics who love their jobs are somewhat protected from the most severe health risks, and this may be because they feel that their work is worth all the hard work, they put in. But this brings up another caveat: Although we found that engaged workaholics

had lower physiological health risks (lower RMS) than non-engaged workaholics, they still reported more depressive feelings, sleep problems, various psycho-somatic health complaints, and a higher need for recovery than non-workaholics (HBR 2018).

These are all signs that well-being among workaholics, regardless of how much they love their job, can be impaired. Mine was impaired. Some statistics which I think are interesting:

Almost half of Americans consider themselves workaholics (Schmall, 2018):

- Fifty-four percent prioritize work before their personal life.
- Fifty-one percent worry about working on a day off.
- Fifty percent struggle to switch off while on vacation.
- Forty-eight percent check emails in the middle of the night.
- Forty-six percent are the first in the office and the last to leave.

Why do we do this to ourselves? Why did I do that to myself? I wanted to succeed at all costs. I wanted to be the best at what I did because it mattered to me that people saw me work hard and get good results. Because somehow, the message I received/interpreted was that this was the only way to get ahead. Please don't misread and believe this was written anywhere but in my head. I still, to this day, feel blessed that I had the career and support along the way.

But I will also say this. No one can stop this insanity but you, or in this case, me. When is enough enough? When can you comfortably have a nicely balanced life where you aren't trying to prove yourself all the time?

Do you want to know the honest answer? The answer is clear as day to me now. You have to believe you deserve success. You must believe you are enough regardless of the hours and wear and tear you put on your body. You must know your worth enough to say no within the confines of your current work and life situation. In other words, you can't just say no to say no. You must have a solid reason for the no that you feel comfortable with.

This whole chapter may sound like an oversimplification. But let's use the shopaholic example for a minute. If you buy too many clothes you can't afford or don't need, you know you must stop, so why is it any different for work? This is all inner work, and I am doing it now. It is challenging and wonderful all at the same time. I had this power all along, but I was never comfortable using it consistently. What would people think of me? Was I not dedicated enough to my company? My clients? My family? After all, I had rationalized for years that I did this *for* my family.

I am conscious of coach-y terms, so I want to help define "*Inner work.*" So many people want a magic wand to help fix themselves, myself included. They come to coaching wanting some sort of change or transformation. But this change really happens from the inside out, and you will see me say this a few thousand times in this book.

First, once you realize you want to change or improve some aspect of your life, you are already winning. Progress first starts with awareness, including noticing your behaviors and why you are doing the things you are doing. In fact, at the beginning of my coaching sessions, I may have someone simply write down when they notice certain behaviors or actions. How often do they use the word should, which is a highly judgmental word, when they are being hard on themselves. I don't necessarily want them to take any action yet. I just want them to pay attention.

Hali came to me unsure of her next career move. She had been nominated and completed the required training to become a partner. She finished the courses and evaluations with flying colors. But she had not been tapped on the shoulder to become a partner. In one of our first sessions, she said she wasn't even sure she wanted to be a partner. There would be too much work, and she valued her quality of life. She did not want to work as much as her current leaders. Hmm... I dug in.

My job is to ask questions, not to give my opinion.

So I asked her, "How much would your job actually change once you become a partner?" Silence.

A long bout of silence here. Hali answered, "I am already doing the job of a partner."

Hali is not alone. We all tell ourselves stories to keep us exactly where we are. That is the evolutionary role of fear—to save us from predators. In this case, the only predator afoot was Hali, who was cannibalizing herself and her chances for partnership because she was scared. Once she realized the stories she was telling herself were not true, we built a plan for the promotion, which included creating a deck with her accomplishments and setting up a time to speak to her bosses to officially raise her hand for the partnership role. I am happy to report that Hali called me to say she is "officially a partner!" She also shared that coaching was one of the "hardest and best things she had ever done." I will take this as a compliment.

Do not wait for anyone to tap you on the shoulder for your next job.
You are in charge of your destiny.

Diving into our true motivations in life is never easy, but it is so worth it. Workaholism hides a multitude of issues and may present as imposter syndrome. Are you afraid someone will find out you aren't as good as the world thinks you are? Or, if you work less, someone else wants it more? There is no ism in this world that isn't a type of parasite robbing the host of some required nutrients.

You can read a plethora of books on why we do the things we do. But the most critical information is your belief in yourself. For workaholics like me, what was I giving up working at this pace? Sleep, quality time with my kids, sleep, peace, and so much more.

I started to understand that the enormous pressure I had always put on myself was not helping me grow. In fact, it was doing the exact opposite. The metrics I used to run my coaching business were undoubtedly important, but I hid behind them. I wasn't being me. I was being the uber coach I thought I was supposed to be. Once I relaxed a little bit more and realized what made me want to coach, I settled in. I focused less on metrics and more on the work I was doing with my clients. And my business grew.

Even as an entrepreneur, where I am solely responsible for my business growth, I am far less stressed. I have a beginning, middle, and end to my workday. I let things roll off me more. I don't worry about the other shoe dropping. I breathe. I am free to run my business the way I want when I want.

I am still wired to be at my desk at a certain time. This is mainly because I am very productive in the morning, but now I have no problem blocking off my calendar to take time for myself. I am vigilant about time blocking my calendar to ensure I created writing time for this book. I am much less worried about the next client, the next dollar, or the next program. I am very focused on delivering every day to my clients. I never in a million years thought I could worry less and still be a successful entrepreneur. Success means different things to different people. It used to mean title and compensation, but today, it represents more freedom, more choices, and a self-sustaining business. It means a business where I can learn and thrive, but it does not own me.

Corporate Operating System:

Stress equals you must be doing it right. Working hard plus being stressed means you are taking your life very seriously, and isn't that what validates success?
Ease equals you are doing it wrong, and you must not care enough.

Coaching Operating System:

Ease equals you are in the moment. You are allowing yourself to pause and think through your life situations.
Stress equals what is your body trying to tell you?

Look, I am not so naive to believe our lives will never be stressful. It is a given that we will all have periods of stress. It is how we deal with stress that can change. Do we need to approach every stressful situation as if the world is going to end, or can we give ourselves a breather and some space to see different perspectives?

Recently, I had a pretty nasty exchange with a close connection. I was distraught and wanted to fight back against the injustice of the written attack. I excused myself from the people I was around, and went to my room to think and breathe. My head was swirling and drowning in a sea of negativity. "Why was all this happening to me?" "This is so unfair." "I must have deserved this." I was making myself feel horrible. I didn't want to feel this way, so what did I do? I got quiet and took some deep breaths. "No, I didn't deserve this attack." "I wasn't going to let it make me suffer." I dusted myself off and returned to my day. The situation didn't change, my reaction to it changed. Do not keep the ball in play because that keeps the exchange going. You do not have to respond to negative interactions right away, if at all.

Maybe you are shaking your head and saying it can't be *that* easy. You can choose how you want to feel, respond, and think. This is the truth that set me free from myself. It is the most important work I have ever done; it is like a muscle that you must exercise regularly to form new patterns. You can do it.

While editing this book, I told my son I would be spending the day working on updates. I told him I was working on a chapter titled "I Am a Recovering Workaholic."

And he said, "Well, you still are."

I was surprised he said this, so I asked, "How so?"

He replied, "You are still working at 9 p.m., editing, and your boundaries are still not crystal clear."

My son is an entrepreneur with his own clothing brand and works *interesting* hours. Sometimes he sleeps until late in the day and works throughout the night. I know I have changed and am not *as much* of a workaholic because I don't dread a phone call, text, or the week ahead. I am less distracted and can shut off my work when I am done for the day. Do I still treat my day like a workday? Yes, I do.

I am also much more likely to meet a friend, make travel plans, and take personal calls during the day, which I did not do in my previous life. To my credit, I did not get on the defensive with my son. I listened and let him tell me his thoughts. Maybe I should list this in my accomplishments file?

It may be hard for others to see your changes, even when you see and feel the changes in yourself. They may need more time to adjust because you have been this way for a very long time. It may be hard for them to embrace the new you. They may be scared you will no longer need them. On the flip side, one of the coolest things about coaching is when my clients tell me others have noticed changes in them.

Just today, a client told me her husband heard her on the phone having some very tough employee discussions. We had worked together earlier in the day to prepare her for her performance review calls. She was nervous because she cares so much, and she was delivering some less than stellar feedback to two of her team members.

Her husband overheard the calls and said, "You sounded great on the calls, very straightforward, transparent, empathetic, and confident."

On a later session with this same client, she said, "I know our last session was tactical around letting people go and reframing that. I'd like to keep digging in on how to grow as a leader." Stop the presses. People management is not tactical. People think that leadership development happens in sweeping, large moments, but it happens in micro moments much more often. When we discussed this further, she said, "I get it now, these are building blocks to greater growth." Yes, building blocks to more confidence, which is the cornerstone of leadership development.

We are all works in progress, but if and when you do the work, it does become easier.

I am living proof, despite what my son said.

CHAPTER 11

THIRTY-THREE AND ME

I have always had an affinity for the number thirty-three. I grew up on 33 Hampshire Avenue, Larry Bird was number thirty-three, and for some reason, it has always felt like my number.

I looked up the significance of the number. Apparently, thirty-three is a master number—meaning teacher—and is generally associated with compassion, inspiration, honesty, discipline, and bravery. I liked where this was going. The number thirty-three tells us "all things are possible." The number thirty-three symbolizes guidance (2016). If you believe in this sort of thing, it is no wonder I have gravitated to coaching.

If you don't believe in this sort of thing, maybe you can admit it is at least interesting. So, stay with me here. I genuinely believe there are signs all around us if we choose to see them. That coincidence is not just a thing but a designed happenstance.

Every year, I think Mother's Day will be just another day. It's a manufactured holiday with some much-needed appreciation for the tireless work of mothers everywhere. And every year, I am wrong. This year was no different, but with an added twist. As I was riding in an Uber, reveling in time with my daughter in Chicago, my childhood neighbor, Denise, sent a picture of my parents from sixty years ago.

Why this weekend? I choose to believe this is one of the small gifts your loved ones who are no longer with you, gift you. A moment when you realize they never truly leave you because they are in your hearts, your children's faces, and forever locked away in your memories. You can certainly live your life believing this is hogwash, but how much sweeter is it to believe our loved ones are always with us in spirit?

I hired a social media person, and she asked me to find some old pictures of me for an upcoming post. I have thousands of photos and saw a picture of my older brother and me dancing at a family event. I stared at this picture for hours and hours because I could see traces of my parents dancing behind us. Even though I see only parts of their faces, I could see they were happy. It warmed my heart. Pictures really do tell a story, don't they?

After a few days, I turned over the picture, and here is what I discovered. The handwritten number thirty-three! I was blown away! I assume this was a proof number in case anyone wanted to order the photo, but I honestly have no idea.

A few weeks later, I traveled for a girls' weekend, and when we checked into our room, I noticed our room number was thirty-three.

My father passed away on March 2, 2022. I started to receive the phone bills for his condo in the Berkshires. The monthly bill total was twenty-five dollars and four cents. This represents the last four digits of our childhood phone number. The next month, the bill was twenty-six dollars and eleven cents.

My final story on how meaningful numbers are to my family and me is a mindblower. My mother died in 1985, two weeks after my middle brother had gotten married and right before the Thanksgiving holiday. My dad loved to play the lottery. Every week, he played two tickets. One ticket was for his children's birthdays, and the other was for he and my mother's corresponding birthdays. He won the lottery on the latter ticket for $14 million, fifteen years after my mom passed away and right before the—drum roll please—Thanksgiving holiday. There are two famous quotes from my dad that are worth sharing. "You have to play to win." And to my mother, who we assumed was behind the magic of winning the lottery, he said, "what took you so long?" I am sure this type of "higher-level" of involvement is frowned upon or else we would all be rich! I wonder if they have house arrests in heaven?

What do the wise sages say about repetitive numbers? Seeing repetitive numbers is a form of synchronicity—a phenomenon described by psychiatrist, Carl Jung, as "*a meaningful coincidence of two or more events where something other than the probability of chance is involved.*" In other words, synchronicity is far more than serendipity, which involves luck and chance. Synchronicity is birthed from the unconscious and etheric realms. In other words, when we experience synchronicity, we are being sent signs and messages from our unconscious minds and higher selves (2022).

I believe in this much more than I realized. I have been trained in intuition by a forensic medium who helps with missing person cases and was a former police officer. I signed up for her course on a whim during COVID-19 because I was trying to fill my time. Who doesn't want to tap more into intuition?

Intuition is a huge part of everyday life and it 1,000 percent includes corporate America. Being able to "read a room," figuring out who the key decision makers are, feeling the energy of your teams and knowing if something is going on without any specific information, and sensing that there are messages clients send without vocalizing them are all examples of intuition. Likewise, you can feel if something is amiss in your family, with your friends, and your relationships. Our job as leaders is to see around corners and predict when an employee or business situation might be at risk. "What's your gut?" is a question I have been asked many times in my career. Thinking is using your head; knowing is using your gut. Intuition equals gut.

How many people trust their intuition?

Fifty percent of Americans trust their gut to tell what's true, and 62 percent of business executives often rely on gut feelings (2017). I had a new boss. I immediately knew I was not on his list of top employees. I could feel it in my bones. There were no words to support my thinking, but feelings are information, and I could not and did not ignore this warning sign. I interviewed a candidate he had referred. I knew I had no choice but to hire this person, and I also knew this person was meant to be my replacement. I told one of my more senior leaders that I had just interviewed my replacement. She ended up intervening only after I had given my notice, and another job was created for me.

Despite my intuition, there were many, many times that I did not say or do the things I wanted to. The sales rep, a.k.a. my replacement, was not a good salesperson and was an even worse manager. I understand he was told he didn't have to worry about selling because he eventually would be taking my job. He and my glorious boss had relatively short stays at the company. Yes, I believe in karma.

I thought I was tapped into my feelings and overall well-being, but I was not. The day I took my last gig in corporate, I was handed a very generous new compensation package, but I felt like I was attending my own funeral. Why didn't I listen to this? Why don't we listen when we get signs clearly meant to guide us?

I interviewed Joanie Gauthier, the holistic healer, for this book. She helped me understand why I was unable to digest salads. She said what she finds with her clients is:

> "Being open is the hardest thing to do. We are ruled by fear and have difficulty with trust—trust in our higher self. We all have intuition, gut responses, and inner knowing. Truth feels different. You can feel the energetic vibration when you are in truth."

I know you have all had the experience of when someone says something that rings true, you may have a physical reaction—goosebumps, hair raising, or a sensation in your body.

Here is how Joanie describes herself: Joanie is an internationally respected holistic practitioner and facilitator with clients across the globe. She assists people on their path of life evolution and holistic health. Joanie has over two decades of experience in the physical Western science of anatomy and physiology and dissection, physical therapy, and alternative therapies, including hand medicine, homeopathic, holistic nutrition, and meditation. She sees you beyond just your physical body. She incorporates mind, body, and spirit because we are spiritual beings living a human existence. And she has helped me grow in so many ways.

Can we bring more spirituality into the workplace where it is desperately needed? How do we even define workplace spirituality? According to Petchsawang and Duchon, workplace spirituality or spirituality at work is defined as "having compassion towards others, experiencing a mindful inner consciousness in the pursuit of meaningful work, and that enables transcendence" (2009). One bit of research: corporate giants like Google, Apple, McKinsey, and Nike, to name a few, have made great efforts to address the spiritual needs of their employees by making mindfulness part of their corporate culture. At its core, mindfulness in the workplace is about developing the ability to be present without judgment or reaction (2022). I believe spiritual health is integral to a healthy workplace. Spirituality at work is becoming an essential aspect of organizations around the world, and for a good reason—its numerous benefits (2022). Here are some of the benefits:

- Improved overall well-being of employees.
- Increased employee productivity.
- Reduced absenteeism.
- Increased motivation and commitment.
- Increased job satisfaction.

- Improved quality of life.
- Increased employee morale.
- Reduced workplace stress.
- Reduced employee burnout.
- Reduced employee turnover rates.
- Improved work performance.

After my initial appointment with Joanie, it took me longer than I wanted to make the changes I wanted and needed to make, but the wheels were in motion. This was important for me to write about because I had this experience of ignoring the warning signs I received. I understand we are always getting messages of some kind, but we choose to ignore many of them. I ignored the signs—insomnia, constant anxiety, always on the go, and never setting proper boundaries in an effort to continue to prove my worth. The very thing I prided myself on, I did not put in practice for myself. Not a new story, but a better ending.

Why? I was afraid to leave a job I was good at, the steady paycheck, and the security and stability of a known entity. Was I good enough to succeed anywhere else? I had some prior evidence to support this answer being no. When I went to the media buying company, I left quickly. When I went on my own, I lasted about two years. You have to be ready, and if you are not, fear may take over. As is fear's primary goal, it kept me right where I was and guided my decisions to keep me safely in the same place. The voices in my head sounded like this:

"Donna, you left before and you didn't make it work, why is this time any different?"

Our thoughts make so much sense, don't they? Why would you not believe this to be true? But you are not your thoughts. You have much more agency over your decisions. Don't be fooled.

My coaching clients come to me because they are in some sort of a transition—wanting to improve their careers/lives, move on, get promoted, or do their jobs to the best of their abilities. Sometimes, they are in need of a new job overall. But they always want some type of change. I don't deal just with the physical aspects of this transition. I can help you with presentation skills and executive presence all day long, but you need to deal with what is happening in your insides to make sustainable changes.

Just today, I was working with a new client who said, "How I am feeling on the inside does not match at all how I am presenting on the outside." At heart, this fantastic client is shy and reserved but feels that if she isn't speaking up in meetings, she isn't leading and won't be as respected as more assertive leaders. She is tired and burnt out and feeling so low. The environment is really sapping her confidence, and it is time for a change. The change doesn't necessarily mean she has to leave the company. We are working on helping her show up differently at work and responding to situations in a more measured manner.

I go deeper with my coaching. I am the facilitator asking the right questions giving you the space to understand yourself at a much deeper level. I help you see that you have the answers inside of you. Success is an inside job. I believe all things are possible. I believe there are signs all around us and in us that help us live our lives more fully—if we pay attention.

What do you believe?

CHAPTER 12

THE GRIEVANCE OF GRIEF

On my first day of my first full-time corporate job, my mother died.

One thing every one of us has in common is that we will lose people we love. This is the cost of living, loving, and being human.

I went in for my first day of work in Boston in beautiful Back Bay and got the call that I had to go to the hospital. This was not a surprise. My mother had been ill for the better part of ten years. We knew this day was coming, but you just always think you have more time.

Fortunately, the hospital was relatively close by. My mother died late that night after a long battle with breast cancer. As a true testimony to her strength, she waited to leave us until my older brother flew in from Louisiana. A few short hours before she died, she was watching *Wheel of Fortune* in the hospital room and guessed one of the final puzzles. She had her whole family around her as she took her last breath. I don't think I will ever forget the sheer beauty and poignancy of this moment.

As was and is the common business practice, I had a week of bereavement leave. I returned to work on the following Monday just as one of my colleagues was returning from her vacation in Hawaii. We had no cell phones or computers back then so there was no way for me to communicate the news before her return to the office. I was not leaving a voice mail message on her home phone.

I don't remember the exact conversation we had, but I am sure I asked her about her trip, and she asked about my week. I told her my mother had passed away. I can visualize the look of total shock on her face, and then her words to me: "What are you doing here?"

Honestly, I don't remember much else from the conversation. But, looking back, what the heck was I doing back at work? I was not even close to being ready to work and pretend like my life hadn't just been turned upside down. I was twenty-two years old living without my mother. I was lost, completely lost.

This time in my life was a blur. I worked and continued working. Working helped me get through my grief or certainly to avoid it. I don't know for sure. Grief is like childbirth. Time protects you from the agony of the event. I do know that lone car rides were my safe crying spots. I lived at home with my dad who had just lost his beloved wife. She was his everything. Yes, they fought, but they also loved deeply. We were a pair, my dad and I, and the sadness and despair in our house was palpable.

I think the juxtaposition of vacation time and bereavement leave is interesting. So much can happen in one week, but the radically different events are treated roughly the same in terms of time off. I happened to work for a small mom-and-pop shop and the owners were like a family to me. I am sure I could have taken more time off, but I was so wet behind the ears, I wouldn't have known to even ask.

Given the times we are living in just a shade after the COVID-19 pandemic, I looked into this further to see what the effects are when a grieving person goes back to work too soon. A *Harvard Business Review* article simply states, "Give more time off" (2020).

Give more time off

Given all the tasks associated with arranging and/or traveling to a funeral, sorting out finances, and mourning one's loss, a few days off from the demands of our jobs doesn't cut it. Organizations need to step up with more paid leave. Facebook set the bar in 2017 when it doubled its bereavement leave to twenty days paid following the loss of an immediate family member and up to ten days for an extended family member. Not coincidentally, COO Sheryl Sandberg lost her husband in 2015 and wrote a book, *Option B*, about the experience (2017).

There is still more work to do. I have seen workers who need time off when a pet passes away. I have seen workers who need time off because they are burned out, have friends who have passed away, who need time simply because the world seems like it is on fire, and they need some safety and time to regroup. Grief comes in all shapes and sizes. And we know that grief is not linear.

One of the ideas I liked was to give a bank of bereavement time so the employee can take the time as they need it—ten days now, maybe ten days later (2020). If COVID-19 has taught us nothing else, it is that people need to feel seen and heard or they will leave ala the great resignation. We should customize benefits; I understand we need guidelines of some sort, but a cookie cutter approach does not work. My last company allowed us to provide the support our employees needed with very little approval needed.

During 2022, right around the time I decided to write this book, my relatively healthy ninety-year-old dad passed away after a too brief illness. There were thirty-seven years between the death of my parents. I always thought I was closer to my mother and romanticized our relationship over these many years, but I honestly don't remember being quite as devastated as losing my dad. Maybe it is because I had my dad around for a lot longer. Maybe it was because although I wasn't as close conversation-wise with my, man of few words, dad, I was always enveloped in his unconditional love. Maybe it is because when you have lost both of your parents, you are faced with your own mortality and the reality that you are now officially, the oldest generation in your family.

Many adult orphans say that while their initial pain and sorrow eased over time, the death of their parents spurred life changes that would never be undone. The most enduring of those changes is the sudden, permanent disappearance of life's familiar backdrop. Levy writes, "Parents provide a unique spot on this planet, which is called 'home,' where we can return, if we need to, to be loved and to feel that we belong. This spot, in the parent's heart and in our mind, has existed from the beginning of our lives, and it has flourished in shared ancestry with roots stretching back to the beginning of time... After parents die, it's gone" (2003).

Thank goodness, during this difficult time, I was no longer in my corporate career. Although I am sure I could have taken as much time off as I needed to manage my dad's illness and death, I would have had work hanging over my head—work I wasn't doing, and work others would have to do in my place. This would have been very difficult for me to handle.

As an entrepreneur, I cleared my schedule as needed. I still coached during this time, but I scheduled less sessions and classes. Yes, I earn less when I work less, but that is a small price to pay for the honor of taking care of your loved ones.

I spent fifty straight days with my dad. From January 10 to March 2, I saw him every single day but one. My brothers and I each had our own roles. I handled the health care and care providers. My oldest brother moved in with me and handled the meal planning and excursions, and my middle brother handled the finances. Each of us visited every day that we were able to and took turns supporting my dad and each other. As with my mother's death, having my brothers around working in unison to manage my dad's death was a lifesaver. No matter where life brings each of us, the love I feel for them is something I can't quite articulate to give it the full merit it deserves. We were able to take care of the person who took care of us the longest and loved us the most.

One of the aides who cared for my dad wrote this:

"I also take the opportunity to appreciate the great children that your dad, Abba, raised. You cared for him selflessly and gave him all the love a child could give to a parent. You fulfilled the fourth commandment, honor your mother and father, a commandment which gives an obligation to children to care for their parents especially in their old age. I was also very pleased to witness the great teamwork and true love that the three of you had and how you worked as ONE to care for Dad. You taught great lessons without a word."

Conversations with my dad were generally one-sided, perhaps because he was hard of hearing in his later years, but regardless, he loved being with his family. Nothing made him happier. And nothing made us happier than to be with him. We had a huge ninetieth birthday celebration planned for him in August 2022 at our family beach house, but COVID-19 and a hurricane threat had other plans. We canceled the party and spent the weekend together with just our immediate family. In our hearts, even before we got the tragic diagnosis, we knew this would likely be his last birthday with us.

So many lessons can be learned here. From a corporate perspective, let your employees decide what they need to do to grieve the way they need to. My old boss lost his father and came to a meeting with me the following week. The funeral was not for another couple of weeks and working kept his mind off the inevitable goodbye. We all grieve and work through grief differently. We may look fine on the outside, but our insides may be hurting deeply. I am not alone in appreciating that there is now more emphasis than ever on mental health.

From a personal perspective, the lessons I learned from my dad, who was not even close to a successful businessman, were many. Showing up and spending time with your loved ones matters. Showing up always matters. He came to every game, every dance recital, and every graduation. I am sure there are a few other parents and grandparents out there who remember the intensity my dad had on the side of a soccer field. Did he ever gently yell at a ref for a bad call? Possibly.

My dad was born before the technology age and never used a cell phone or a computer. When he was with you, he was present. There really is no better gift than this. This type of presence is hard to find in our world of too much connectivity. To keep my dad in touch with all his grandchildren, I bought my dad an iPad, which he loved. Facebook was his jam, and he commented on posts like nobody's business and always liked to tell me about his comments with a smile on his face and a giggle on his lips. He loved Facebook. Unfortunately, he eventually forgot how to use this tool and forgot his passwords more times than I can recount. But for the time he did use Facebook, it was an absolute joy for us and so much fun for him. Except for the time he posted comments on a spam post, and my email was connected to his account. I must have gotten a thousand emails that day.

If I can tell one more story about my dad, it is to showcase his amazing sense of humor and quick wit. After significant family pressure by my children—specifically my son who passed a bill in Massachusetts for animal rights (HB344 Logan's Law) where you can no longer devocalize your pets—I succumbed to the pressure of adopting a dog. We agreed we would adopt an older dog, providing more like hospice care, because they were less likely to be adopted. We adopted a small terrier mix who was appropriately named Scruffy. Before long, we learned Scruffy was deaf, going blind, and incontinent. He began walking into walls and stopping in place. It wasn't a pretty sight. One day, my dog-loving dad was over at the house and saw this in action and said, "your dog needs a seeing eye dog." Hilarious right?

My dad was not the most confident man. He lived through his children and probably got the biggest ego boost when my oldest brother went to MIT. He loved my middle brother and me very much, but for a man who thought less of himself and his intelligence, MIT was a validation of his parenthood at a whole other level. One day, my dad's temple gave him the "Man of the Year Award" for his generosity and commitment to the community. I don't think I have ever seen him so happy. It was a day about him and his abilities, not his children's. He deserved that. We all do. But, yes, he did raise three confident successful children. My brothers are solid upstanding men who love their families. I ended his eulogy with these Hebrew words, Yasher Koach, which meant "good job, you done good, Dad."

Here is what has nurtured me through the grieving process:

- Talking about my dad with my family and other people who loved him.
- Making him part of my everyday life as opposed to a taboo "don't want to upset you so let's not talk about him" subject.
- Keeping pictures of him around me.
- Going to his favorite place and sitting in his favorite chair.
- I made donations to his favorite charities—put a plaque up in his honor.
- When I am with my friends, I ask them to tell me something they remember about my dad.

Okay, one more story. The week before my dad died, we took him to brunch. He was very frail and in a wheelchair. The restaurant served coffee in gigantic mugs, and it was too heavy for him to lift, so he asked for a crane to go with his coffee. And because humor seems to run in the family, my older brother poured his coffee into the small creamer at the table. How I love and miss this man. How I wish I could hear him say my name again, feel his giant hugs, and hold his hand.

At the end of 2022, my oldest brother had a heart attack while in mid-speech on a stage in New York City followed by a massive stroke and blood clot. He is well on his way to a full recovery! He is sixty-four-years old and my BFF. I spent the last two months of 2022 by his side. I almost wrote that I had given up the last two months of 2022 to be with him. No, it is not giving up time. It is spending time with the people I care about most. I will never regret it.

And you will never regret shutting down your laptop early, going to your kids' games or events, or taking time off.

You will only regret the things you did not do. You will also regret not spending as much time with the people you loved because you let too many other things get in the way.

CHAPTER 13

NO ONE DOES IT ALONE

Everyone has heard the phrase that behind every successful man is a strong woman.

But what about successful women building each other up?

"Behind every successful woman is a tribe of successful women who have her back."

"Surround yourself with women who would say your name in a roomful of opportunities!"

"Have a mentor," said the coach.

I have had the good fortune of having both good men and women guide me along the way.

At my first post-college job, I had Barb Gibson and Marlene Nussbaum. Marlene was one of the owners of the small agency I worked for. She was a beautiful, intelligent woman who had everything I aspired to in my life. She had a great job where she was highly successful, a husband, three beautiful children, beautiful clothes, and an executive presence long before I knew what this even was. Barb was the picture of grace, intelligence, and wit. Everyone loved her, and she always knew just what to say and do.

Early in my career, I was working on a client issue and got into a heated argument with a publication. I was getting very animated and loved a good scrappy fight back then.

Marlene happened to be walking by and heard me. She asked me what was going on, and I told her. For the life of me, I don't remember what the actual issue was, but likely the publication forgot to publish a scheduled advertisement. I was so proud of myself for dealing with the situation, but then, *boom!*

The next sentence changed my life.

"You are solving the wrong problem, Donna."

She was right. I was so caught up in the moment and focused on winning that I never considered that I had lost sight of the original issue. I live with these words in my head to guide me every day.

Marlene was also the picture of grace in some challenging situations. She was one of three partners at our ad agency, and she led our sales team. The other two were very close, almost uncomfortably so. This other female partner, who I also admired but not quite as a role model, was everything Marlene was not. She was single, attractive, but not Marlene-level, and more of an inside operations person. This trio of partners must not have been easy to manage, but Marlene never said a word.

Many years later, a small group of us got together and reminisced. Marlene finally shared how challenging it was to work with the other two, but she found her place with them, and they even ended up starting another company together. Every day, she went to work in what must have been like enemy territory, and every day, she figured out a way to make it work.

I keep in touch with Marlene. I randomly sent her a note about how much she has meant to me in my career. This is part of what she wrote me back:

"I love seeing the pictures of you and your family. The love you all have for each other tugs at my heart. You are a great mother.

From the day I met you, I knew you were special. You have Integrity, an incredible work ethic, and a zest for life."

Maybe she was just being kind, but the words mean so much to me coming from someone I so admire. Everyone needs a Marlene as a mentor.

Barb Gibson was my peer. She was a level above me when I started, and she could do no wrong. Her clients loved her. Getting a compliment from Barb was like winning the lottery. As kind as she was, she was also demanding because she cared deeply about the work we delivered to our clients. She expected top notch service from us, and I learned by osmosis what I wanted to be like on the client and sales side. At our company, we were responsible for both sales and service, and no one did it better than Barb. She also had a large map on her office wall with red pushpins of all the places she had traveled. I was in awe, and it is still something we laugh about today.

Barb put her whole heart and soul into her client relationships. I remember seeing Barb crying outside of our offices under the large circular arches on Congress Street. She had been told by her biggest account that they would be leaving the agency, and she had to tell the head partner. Even he was not angry with Barb when he saw how upset she was. She was already beating herself up enough. It was one of the few times I saw this man display empathy. There are always situations that are beyond our control, but that doesn't mean it doesn't hurt like heck.

Barb and I recently had breakfast together. We reminisced about our agency life, specifically about the above event.

Often, it felt like there was very little loyalty. I can't say I disagree with Barb on this topic. It is hard to give so much of yourself to your work and not feel some anger when you lose a client or deal. But that is part of doing business, and I have come to understand that despite our feelings, business is sometimes just business. It has never prevented me from giving my all, though, because that is what I am responsible for.

This job provided great mentors, learning, tools, and opportunities to advance my career. I was like a sponge soaking up every minute, watching and learning from the people around me. Advertising was loaded with women, so I was always surrounded by capable, inspiring women.

What are the benefits of a positive mentoring relationship?

Maybe you're fresh out of school and looking to begin your career, or perhaps you've already established yourself within your chosen profession. If want to continue your climb up the corporate ladder, then finding and fostering a relationship with a mentor should be seen as an essential step on your road to success (2020).

A good mentor can assist you in your personal and professional development—essentially, helping you realize your full potential.

Here are some of the benefits of having a mentor:

- Help guide you toward reaching your career goals.
- Provide encouragement as you pivot throughout your career.
- Offer honest feedback.

- Help you navigate office politics.
- Help with salary negotiations.
- Hold you accountable to the goals you have set out for yourself.
- Help you do your job better.
- Champion your development.
- Help you network.
- And so much more.

Managers can be mentors, but generally managers are more focused on having you succeed in your current role. If you have a manager who also operates like a mentor, you are very fortunate. You can have mentors both at and outside of your place of employment. Most mentors would be honored to know you selected them to help you.

According to statistics compiled by Sun Microsystems in a study following one thousand employees over five years, those who received mentoring were 20 percent more likely to get a raise than their peers who chose not to participate. Additionally, mentees were promoted five times more often than those employees without mentors. This benefit alone should provide all the justification needed to seek out a workplace mentor (2007).

But, because we're all about receiving raises, a mentor can also offer guidance before you begin negotiating your future employment contracts. The insight a mentor can provide will help empower you to negotiate for the biggest salary increase and best benefits package possible. (2020). Clearly, having a mentor will give you an edge over your competition.

Finally, it's worth noting that most mentees—89 percent, according to research—eventually become mentors. This statistic speaks volumes about how rewarding these relationships can be. So, if you want to achieve greater levels of success while simultaneously speeding up your climb to the top, find a mentor and make it happen (2017).

I have worked at and with companies that provide mentorship. The results speak for themselves, but I can't say I have seen all companies stay on top of the programs. Given the times we live in with the "great resignation," "quiet quitting," and all the other business terms, mentoring feels like a win-win to create excellent employee engagement. This single and simple act of having a mentor would most certainly reduce employee turnover at both the mentor and mentee levels.

Client Relationship Skills

Advertising didn't pay well. I worked weekends at a custom-order stationery store filled with interesting women to make ends meet. Once I started working with clients at the agency and the stationery store, my network began to grow. I didn't know it at the time, but my client work was the best possible training for my career. I learned to watch and learn how clients responded to situations. One agency client called and sang a song to me when he fell in love with our creative concepts. Another client threw the creative we presented across the room—classy, huh? I learned I could start anticipating client needs from observing, though I didn't anticipate the torque of the throwing arm of the client I just mentioned.

My client skills are perhaps my strongest skill, earning me the Top Client Service Person in the World award at my last company. I am very proud of the work I have done and continue to do.

Interviewing My Clients

I interviewed two of my favorite clients for this book. They have had a profound and lasting impact on me.

One is Bill, and I am 1,000,000 percent certain there is no finer person on the planet. Bill always stayed with me as the leader I wanted to be. He was kind to everyone. He was smart, respectful, and not afraid to have a little fun. He would rarely, if ever, consider getting angry with anyone because he is a true gentleman. He summed it up this way, "I would push the pause button and reflect before responding." What a smart man.

I told him he left an indelible imprint on me. In our discussion, he said, "I believe in praising in public and punishing/providing feedback in private." I cannot tell you how many times I have seen leaders berate their employees in public.

For so many reasons, Bill is a role model for me. He lost his adopted and beloved son to a drug overdose. I went to the wake with my mentor and friend, Barb Gibson. Bill did not skirt around the issue of his son's passing. He wanted to help others, even when he and his wife, Jean, were in the depths of their own pain.

I also interviewed Susan, who has been my mentor since the day I met her. It was her first month of work, and she was tasked with running advertising agency reviews. She knew very little about this field of recruitment advertising, but being the consummate marketing professional she was, she ran the review fairly and asked great questions. For some reason, she took a liking to me, and we have been friends for over twenty-five years. What I admired so much about Susan is that she, like Bill, was always straightforward and honest. It was not her way to attack or threaten us in any way, even when we made mistakes. By threatening, I mean threatening to take business elsewhere. She respected her vendors and treated us all as partners.

There is a big difference between being treated as an interchangeable vendor and a trusted partner. Susan was always accessible and quick to respond when we needed her, despite her position at the company. She was and is loyal to her team. When I interviewed her for the book, she shared her experience at her first big job. She was hired in a marketing communications role at a financial services institution.

One thing Susan loved about this job was that she had a big desk and drawers. She noticed some of the female administrative support staff support would not, in fact, support her because she had, you guessed it, a big desk—no offers to help her with work or onboarding. She managed to be successful, which is no surprise, but later found out the firm had a slight issue with the Equal Employment Opportunity Commission (EEOC). The company told her she was doing a great job and offered her a promotion. Still, she realized the opportunities and additional money they were offering didn't feel authentic, and she stayed for maybe another six months.

She quickly learned that women didn't have as much opportunity to use their voices, and she decided to ensure she helped other women. She could have stayed at the first company and enjoyed the financial perks, but she chose to move on and ensure she helped others. Her integrity shines through with every interaction. Some of her team members, who I met in 1996, are still with her today.

My greatest mentor of all was the CEO of my former company. Her brain works at the speed of light. She can see way beyond the current playing field and is sharper than anyone I have ever met. With all this sharpness comes some thorns; she can be tough and cut you at the knees with a simple raise of an eyebrow. Yet she engenders enormous loyalty with her team because she has a huge heart and a gift for taking care of her team. It was one of the most complex and interesting relationships I have ever had—a little bit of fear mixed with an enormous amount of respect. She provided me opportunities to grow at every turn. I would not be the professional I am today without her support and belief in my abilities.

Sometimes, all it takes is for someone to believe in you and see things in you that you don't even see yourself. That is what I love most about being a coach. I see the greatness in you even when you don't see it in yourself. I am your champion every step of the way.

Although I have outlined some of the tremendous mentors I have had, I hope I have also been a mentor to many others. At the latter end of my corporate career, I did mentor women for a program called Women Unlimited. I credit this program for helping me on my path to coaching. It was the first time I actively gave back outside of my company, and it lit a fire in me to do more. I've had too many days of working, momming, and not much else.

One thing I wanted to spend more time on in this book is asking the people I worked with if and how I impacted them.

One of my favorite employees and people, for too many reasons to count, was and is an absolute dream team member. I finally had the opportunity to work directly with her on one of the largest accounts we had at the agency. She already worked on the account in a media capacity, but we moved her from Atlanta to New York City to run the whole account. It was a massive move for her and her family, and she did it with amazing grace. Moving your husband, dogs, and two small children to another city cannot be easy, all while working at a crackerjack pace.

This was one of the most demanding clients I have ever worked with. Their reputation was legendary within the agency. A meeting with them took hours of prework, all the while knowing we would be thrown a curveball or two regardless of our preparation. I have never seen anyone handle a client's barrage of questions with such grace as Sylvia. She never lost her patience because she understood this client was trying to absorb the information, always looking for a deeper why. I still use a famous quote from this client: "what is the so what of this information?" The client is right. I have learned so much from them. I never present information if I don't understand the details of the information I am presenting. There are gifts of learning everywhere.

Sylvia was the ying to my yang. She could do the math and organize details that would take me a lifetime and then some to learn. She could dive deep into data and explain almost anything. She is very detail-oriented and cares deeply about what she does and the people she works with. Very rarely does one person possess all these qualities, but she does. And then, unexpectedly, cancer hit. She had developed stage four colon cancer.

She called me when I was visiting my son in Pittsburgh, which I thought initially was odd because she no longer worked on my team. It was late, and I remember sitting in bed in a quirky hotel room in shock. I was devastated. How could this be true? How she handled this massive blow is nothing short of astonishing. Pre-COVID-19, I was able to fly and be by her side when she had one of her largest surgeries. She is not completely cancer free and just recently had her sixth surgery within five years. She is a badass woman, and cancer doesn't stand a chance against her.

Making a Difference

Her words about our working relationship are below:

Words Matter

"I know you got this phrase from our chief legal counsel, but you said it when I was being looser than I should have been with my language. At that time in my career, I thought I wasn't overly worried about precise communication, which is funny, coming from someone who always has to do the math. In our discussions, you helped me see that taking a bit more thought ahead of time would not only reduce the potential for misunderstanding, but also improve my executive presence. I think the phrase might have been something like, 'if you said it to our CEO that way, she would come unglued!'"

Transition Review

Here's the bigger one—when I was moving back from NY to ATL, you took the time to do a review that was more like an exit discussion from my old job and work to set me up for success in my new one. While I was technically taking a lateral move with the same job title, you helped me take the opportunity to see what I did well and think through "if I knew then what I know now," I would do differently. Once you're in the pattern, it's hard to break it, and you helped me use the move as a chance to break the pattern and learn from my history.

- *I was super focused on the clients but not enough on the team cohesiveness and development. There was not enough structure around consistent meetings, and I missed opportunities to bring the group together and help them collectively improve their jobs. I was ok with my 1:1s but leaned more on seeing people in the office rather than structured meetings. Fast forward: I was good in the new role, and now I'm extremely disciplined about this because if I'm not, I know it slips through the cracks.*
- *Delegation—I wasn't great at making time to teach others how to do the difficult/quirky things that I historically owned. I also had a challenge trusting that people would do it my way. Fast forward a few months, and I was better but still not great. Then… cancer. Man, having a couple of surprise medical leaves sure reaffirms that you should never be the only one who knows how to do something. Now—it's still a work in progress, but I can say that I've gotten much better about it.*
- *Less emotion—more practicality/problem-solving. You helped me strike a balance. I still get really positive responses from people because they know that I genuinely care—about them, their clients, and their lives. But it's not SO personal anymore. Not that there aren't still moments, but it's far less. At the risk of sounding kitschy, you helped me find the balance between leading with my heart and the needs of the business. That was not always easy for me to find.*
- *You are the definition of a mentor and inspirational leader— well before the transition to coaching began. Rereading what you wrote to me… there is something about this, even after the less emotion comment, that makes my heart swell and puts tears in my eyes.*
  - *"Keep learning, keep growing, and keep being you. You have grown so much—less emotional and more practical—better problem-solving skills and providing*

solutions overall. I am so proud of you and happy that you and your family are back home. I am always here for you."

One of my clients is a twenty-nine-year-old stage four head and neck cancer survivor. I have known her since she was in first grade. Her mother called me one day and asked, "Can you help my daughter?" She had 90 percent of her tongue removed, was not able to eat solid foods, and had gone through rigorous treatments of radiation and chemotherapy.

What could I do to help her?

Her mother wanted me to work with her to figure out what she wanted to do next. It was unlikely she would be going back to her previous career of personal training. We had our first meeting at a local park. It was better for Abbey to walk and talk for her sessions. Moving her body gives Abbey the most comfort and peace.

We realized quickly that her career was not going to be our starting point. She had gone through so much trauma that she needed a safe space to be a place where she didn't need to make everyone around her feel better as is her nature —a place to mourn for all she had lost.

Slowly, Abbey transformed in front of my eyes. Not just from coaching, but from the whole process of healing and being loved as fully as she is. She started to eat solid foods, adopted another dog, and her body started to get stronger. Her life was returning to a new normal. Then, a total surprise. She became pregnant. A miracle baby if there ever was one.

She was asked to speak at Harvard Medical School at their Grand Rounds. This was the first time ever that a patient has done so. She spoke for over a half hour to the medical staff, doctors, interns, students, and families about her experience. Her main message was to treat the whole patient, not just the medical aspects.

During her beautiful speech, she added that her healing/mental health journey included our coaching.

I asked her questions that set her mind at rest. I had given her space to mourn, cry, vent, heal, and grow.

You don't often realize the affect you have on others. I frequently say that coaching is an honor, but I don't think this word adequately describes the depth of how working with a client and seeing them change feels. You feel like a parent watching your child's first baby steps. It is one of the most magical feelings to know you have impacted each other's lives so profoundly. And, Abbey, she is changing the world.

The year of 2022 was challenging. I started the new year with COVID-19. My dad was diagnosed with pancreatic cancer and died soon after. My partner of twenty-two years and I decided to redefine our relationship with the first step of having him move out of our home, and finally, my older brother had a massive heart attack and stroke from which he is now recovering.

I have accepted a host of support from my friends, family, and kids, which is a new operating system for me. They have listened to me ruminate about the whys and what-ifs more times than I can count. They have supported any decision I have made without judgment, and they have let me cry when that is the only thing I can manage. I hope you have people like this in your life. Let them take care of you. I know you would be there for them in a heartbeat.

Perhaps my next book will be about this poignant period of loss and what I have learned and gained, but right now, I am still a little raw. I know I will make it through this time and land firmly on the other side. My life will continue, my work will continue, and I will find a new way to thrive in a brand-new paradigm of life.

There is no way to go through a grieving or life-changing period without feelings. The more you accept them and let yourself actually feel them, the greater the healing potential. I wish I had a different answer here, but just know that the pain does eventually lessen.

CHAPTER 14

THE COST OF CHANGE

I have been on this earth for 21,535 days. My dad was alive for 21,292 of them, and my mother just 8,030. I spent 12,775 of my days in a corporate job. I have spent 10,220 days as a mother, and 8,030 of these days were spent in a long-term loving relationship. If you believe, like I do, that there are signs all around us, yes, the 8,030 number for both my relationship and my mother seems significant.

Just to keep the math going, I have worked over 80 percent of my life, and over 60 percent of this time has been spent in a corporate setting.

However, the numbers are sometimes less straightforward when making life changes.

In the past, I always thought about change in terms of gains. When I lose ten pounds, this will be a positive. When I start to run, one mile will turn into two miles and so on. It never occurred to me that my life would feel like it was falling apart by changing myself. I just didn't realize that with change comes loss.

If you leave a job, you may either have to get another one and/or get used to another company and job. Even though it is likely a good change to further your career, there is some sense of loss when leaving the comfort of knowing what to expect and the familiarity of your workplace and workmates.

Leaving a relationship that no longer works for you is very similar. "The devil you know" conversation may play out in your head.

"I have to go out and find someone else."

"I don't want to be alone."

"This relationship isn't *so* bad."

"I will never find someone who understands me like he/she/they did."

If you do decide to leave, you undoubtedly will feel the newness of being alone, perhaps attempting to find someone new all the while remembering the more beautiful moments you had. Maybe you will also feel relieved.

I can relate to both of these points because in the past several years, I have left the comfort of a great company and paycheck to forge my own path. I also left the comfort of a long-term relationship, not because parts of it weren't wonderful, but because parts of it needed to change in order for both of us to grow.

Why, though, do we stay in places and spaces we have outgrown? One word—*fear*. Fear beautifully disguises itself in much of the rhetoric that keeps you in the same place.

FEAR (False Evidence Appearing Real)

We all may have heard that the fight/flight response is rooted in evolution—helping to keep us safe. Besides saving us from monstrous predators, fear insidiously works its way into our everyday lives.

Fear can sound like this:

"I have to stay at this job because I have to feed my

family and probably won't be able to get another job that pays like this."

Or it can show up like this:

"I don't want to get too excited about this opportunity if it doesn't work out."
"I don't want the promotion anyway because it will probably be too much work."
"I should be grateful for my relationship. There are so many relationships that are worse than mine."

You want to take a course, but you tell yourself that you haven't studied in years and need to be equipped to take the course—code for not smart enough. Fear sucks the life out of us, and I want to help you breathe it back in.

Here are some steps you can take if you don't want fear to continue to underwrite your life.

Four Steps You Can Take to Help Wrangle Your Fear

1. **Stop should-ing on yourself.**
   Should-ing equals judging yourself harshly.
   Which is more likely to happen?
   "I should go to the gym."
   or
   "I want to go to the gym."
   Our words are powerful detractors or motivators. Pay attention to your word choices.

2. Interrupt your negative thoughts because they rarely support your bravery.

When you hear yourself going kamikaze on your psyche, stop the infighting. Is there a competition for how long you can beat yourself up? In *this* competition, you would win hands down.

"I should be further along in my career." Not supportive.

Stop yourself from spiraling, and ask "I wonder what is going on here?"

This simple break can stop the havoc in your brain.

Sometimes, I take a deep breath and put my hand over my heart. This pause works wonders.

3. Question the validity of the story you are telling yourself.

Is it true that you don't deserve this promotion? If you are afraid of rejection—and who isn't?—your brain will hack you in any way it can. You have the power to stop this nonsense.

"I will never get the promotion."

"So and so deserves it more and has a better relationship with the hiring manager, and so on"

Is this really true? Not likely.

If you don't apply for the promotion, you have zero chance of getting the job.

"Who deserves the promotion more than you?"

4. Change your mindset.

This is the difference between a fixed and growth mindset.

Fixed: I get the job, or I don't. Win-lose scenario.

Growth: If I don't get the job, what did I learn from this experience?

In practice: "I will go for the promotion, and even if I don't get the job, I put myself out there and will be more ready for the next opportunity."

For my first years out of corporate, I paid close attention to my fear because doing new things, such as starting a new business in a new field during a pandemic, will kick your anxiety into overdrive. I did not want fear making decisions for me. I had done this for long enough. Hiring my own coaches helped me to keep taking action regardless of my fear of failure.

Once I acknowledged my fear, but took action anyway, I noticed the changes I was making. I started writing down all the things I had accomplished, and I was like, "whoa, you go girl!" I was not used to being my own cheerleader, and it felt good!

Keeping track of your accomplishments is not only a brag sheet, but a record of how much can happen right before your eyes. Pay closer attention. Like me, you probably don't give yourself nearly enough credit for the work and things you do accomplish. I would like that to stop for you today!

Make a list, it will assist

Everything on the list below is something I am responsible for.

- I left the comfort and reliability of a corporate job.
- I had no next job lined up.
- I signed up for the iPEC Coaching Certification program.
- I passed the coaching exam and am now a PCC (over five hundred hours of coaching).

- I sat for two additional certifications through iPEC—leadership and transition coaching.
- I was an ambassador for new members for ICF International Coaching Federation.
- I hired two coaches—a business and a mindset coach.
- I hired a bookkeeper, a social media manager, and a LinkedIn coach to help me take my business to the next level.
- I created a biweekly email three years ago and have continued to grow my following.
- I created three group coaching programs.
- I established partnerships and programs with people I had never met before.
- I took a class on neuroscience for business at MIT.
- I switched financial planners to one aligned with my family.
- I ended some friendships that were no longer constructive.
- I reestablished friendships with some long-lost friends.
- I built a coaching and consulting business from scratch.
- I took intuition classes during COVID-19 with a forensic medium.
- I started to go to therapy again after my dad's passing.
- I will publish my first book in 2023.
- I sold my house during COVID-19.
- My twenty-two-year relationship changed.

In my group and private coaching sessions, I strongly encourage my clients to keep a list of their accomplishments. I encourage you to do the same. It will help reinforce how valuable you are just the way you are. If you are in corporate, it will help keep you on track from a personal and professional development standpoint. It is beneficial in your one-on-ones with your manager and your regularly scheduled performance reviews, as well as upcoming interviews.

I didn't take my human/soft skills seriously enough because they have always come so naturally to me. I discounted how quickly I could read people even though I know what a critical skill it is.

Being someone who seemingly can "do it all" finally came to a head for me. I can't do it all. No one can. This is the conundrum of being an assertive woman; people assume you must be getting what you want because you are so forthright in other areas of your life, but this wasn't the case for me. It does not appear that I am alone.

As I slowly transitioned to less go go go and more ease ease ease, I realized how much I had been missing in my life and how much I had been tolerating. When you move at the speed of light, you miss seeing the beauty around you. Without going on and waxing poetic, my relationships started to change. Some relationships got better, some got worse, and some were eliminated altogether.

Relationship Woes

My relationship with my partner of twenty-two years had so many positive aspects and so much love. He was the dreamer, and I the pragmatist. He took such great care of me, but we had some huge underlying issues that I often overlooked because I felt I should be grateful for having someone love me so much. We enjoyed each other and were integrated into each other's lives. We fit together.

Because I was so busy in my corporate life, I chose not to deal with the issues. I was pretty frustrated at times with the choices I made, and I took it out on him. He said that sometimes I treated him like he worked for me. I could be dismissive, and I put everything and everyone above him. I made plenty of mistakes in my relationship. We both did.

When I left my corporate career, I said, "It is your turn" because I had been carrying a larger financial share in our relationship for quite some time. His turn did not come, and with the death of my dad and some difficult financial situations for him, things continued to deteriorate. My world was rocked because I was so used to having my dad as the catch-all in my life. I was more vulnerable and unsteady than I can ever remember. I realized I was on my own. It was time to make some changes.

I found two boot camp-type therapists to help get us back on track. It really helped. We had never gotten along better, and it opened us up to learning how we each ticked. We were cooking! But the financial issues continued, and I knew I could no longer ignore that I was a big part of the problem. I had enabled him for far too long.

At the end of the day, his need to drive business success overrode his love for me. He was unwilling to make any substantial changes because he believed he had finally found his thing. Sometimes the greatest love of all is letting people and things go. Love does not conquer all. The ability to change and grow together with love conquers all.

Even with all my life experiences and training, I had not acted on the signs or feelings in my body at work or at home. Why was this relationship good enough for me when I was not getting what I wanted? I turned that mirror on myself and could no longer ignore the situation. This is one of the toughest decisions I have ever made in my life, and I still don't know how this story ends. Good decisions don't always equal good feelings.

I am no different than my clients going through life and work transitions. What are my clients tolerating in their lives? What sustainable changes do they want to make? What is holding them back from living the lives they truly desire? The client always knows what is best for them. My job is to facilitate by asking the right questions.

My dad's death clearly made me see things differently and question my life choices. Was I living the life I wanted to live? Was I with the person I wanted to be with? What were my dreams?

Thankfully, I am a strong, financially independent, successful woman. I knew part of my healing and growth meant I needed my own help. I went back to my pre-COVID-19 therapist to help me through my grief as well as my relationship challenges. She started out as our couple's counselor and was well aware of our issues. I realized I wanted to start fresh, and I found a new therapist after a few months. I had energy healers work on me as well. I had an army of them because I wanted to return to the land of the living and be the healthiest version of myself for my clients, my family, and myself. The pain was intense. I knew there was no way to expedite this process, even though I desperately wanted to. Love does not wash away easily, if at all.

What I do know is that I am enormously capable of any changes I want to make. So are you.

Not only have I leaned on professional help, but also on my family and friends. Initially, it was so uncomfortable to need and ask for love and support, but I got it back in spades. We are not used to receiving because we are so programmed to give of ourselves to others. Think about this like breathing in and out. The in-breath is giving, and the out-breath is receiving; they are part of life's natural flow and rhythm.

You are not weak for asking for help; you are vulnerable and strong for doing so. We have to get more used to seeing vulnerability and strength as co-partners. This was one of the hardest lessons I learned from my mindset coach, and it may be the single greatest lesson I have learned in recent years. People want to help you through your pain. You just need to ask for it. As Brené Brown says, "We don't have to do all of it alone. We were never meant to" (2015).

Here is what Deepak Chopra has to say about receiving:

"Receiving is necessary and important. While giving feels wonderful, it only works when there is a receiver. Allowing yourself to be a gracious receiver is a humbling experience and is truly an act of love because it offers a chance for others to give.

The importance of receiving is not about expecting others to give to you because you are more important or deserving. It is about receiving a gift without guilt or neediness, and without feeling obliged to give back.

How you receive is just as important to the giver's happiness as it is to your own. To receive in a good way requires you to do away with the negative thoughts and instead pause and reflect on the exchange and what it means: friendship, support, love, etc. This fuels a great deal of happiness in both the giver and receiver" (2019).

Thank you for sharing this book journey with me.

I wish you the ability to use your voice more powerfully so you can live the life you so definitely deserve.

I wish you could see yourself through the eyes of the people who love you the most. Believe them.

Mostly, I wish you peace—and fun. Don't ever forget this part.

CHAPTER 15

LET'S CONTINUE THE CONVERSATION

I hope this book gave you a good sense of who I am as a person and how I coach.

Here's a little bit more information about me:

I had a storied career in corporate America working with Fortune 500 companies at the leading independent advertising agency in the world focused on talent and technology. But I was never really happy; I was unsuccessfully successful. I could never really pinpoint the root of my unhappiness, but it never left my side. Still, I am proud of my career. I accomplished more than I ever thought was possible. I learned so much and created long-lasting friendships. In fact, some of my agency clients have become my coaching clients. My mission in life is to help my clients see what is possible.

I help guide ambitious, corporate professionals of any age, at any stage, through the process of self-discovery to create sustainable personal growth and make meaningful life changes. I have helped clients secure jobs, get promoted, reduce conflicts at work, improve executive presence, prepare for performance reviews and interviews, leave jobs to start new ventures, build stronger teams, gain more confidence, and so much more.

We'll work from the inside out, helping to develop your true confidence and establish an unshakable belief in the power of yourself.

I am direct and straightforward. I will coach and guide you with my thirty plus years of experience in corporate America.

My personal mantra is, "say it like it is."

Working with me will help open you up in new ways. It will help you grow and learn more about yourself. It will help you become successfully successful.

You will change.

I can't wait to meet you.

Say it like it is,
Donna

Where to find me

- Website: www.dstarconsultants.com
- LinkedIn: https://www.linkedin.com/in/dstarcoaching/
- Instagram: https://www.instagram.com/dstarconsultants/
- Book a call with me: https://calendly.com/dstar-coaching/what-do-you-really-want

ACKNOWLEDGMENTS

I wrote this book at the tail end of COVID-19 after having written biweekly emails for over three years. This gave me the confidence to make the leap to write this book. You never know how one action can lead to a completely different future.

I have so many people to thank for this experience. First, let me thank Jeffrey St. Laurent for his gentle push to get me to start writing. I want to thank all the people associated with The Book Creator's Group, which is now called Manuscripts. Eric Koester, you are the beacon of how programs should be organized and run. Shanna Heath, thank you for taking a bowl full of newbie writers and helping to mold us into authors—no small feat. To my editors, Angela Mitchell, Megan Hart, Sherman Morrison, a.k.a. the citation guru, and Jacques Moolman, Marketing partner extraordinaire. From soup to nuts, everyone in the Manuscripts program has been outstanding.

Mostly, I want to thank my family and friends, specifically my kids, Hannah and Jordan, for supporting and putting up with me through this process. To my brothers, Jerry and Matthew, I love you. To my friends and family, I could not do this without you. And, to my departed dad, thank you for your unshakable belief in me.

To the people who pre-bought this book and helped me along the way, thank you!

To my beta readers—Shereen, Cindy, Beth, Ellen, Jimmy, Nicky, Meredith, Hannah, Jordan, Matthew, Jerry, Tracy— so much gratitude to you!

Judy Pelletier
Jennifer Spriggs
Lynn Stewart
Cheri Zunick
Barbara Gibson
Cindy Guiness
William Nicholson
Marcy Kublin
Meredith Guiness
Sylvia Kuck
Michelle Mclaughlin
Melissa Frank
Matthew Appelstein
Susan Collins
Lauren Turner
Dana Shkolny
Karen Pollack
Ashley Elich
Tamsin Bencivengo
Karen Long
Alissa Story
James Young
Emily Geller
Abbey Bergman
Jenn Brinn

Ellen Neary
Beth Quenzel-Sherman
Kelli Tungate
Jamie Cerniglia
Tracy Sullivan
Caitlin Medalie
Karen Greenberg
Ellenmarie Rhone
Larry Pelletier
Danielle Leach
Jill Glick
Sharon Margulies
Monica Ferreira
Laura Velasquez
Denise Heitmann
Andrea Ellen
Carol Agranat
Megan Stanish
Jeffrey St. Laurent
Hannah Austin
Jennifer Sheffield
Sara Miller-Paul
Lee McCarthy
Val Moore
Julie Fennell

Ardeshir Mehran
Lesley Decanio
Elaine Faria
Jordan Star
Lisa Kliman
Lisa Gordon
Lynda Picard
Angela Osborn
Maylen Rafuls Rosa
Hannah Star
Kathleen Gilligan
Tricia McCormack
Maryalice Sosnoski
TJ Dinsmoor
Amy Schupler Veaner
Julia Coto
Annette Tuccelli
Sarah Beavins
Marianne Kulka

Sylvie Dore
Shereen Jacobs
Margie Peters
Marlene Nussbaum
Gerald Appelstein
Richard Levin
Julie Goodman
Susan Cruickshank
Raymond Lheureux
Hilary Potts
MaryAnn Higgins
Karen Mindy Gold
Alison Cook-Beatty
Sean Murphy
Jamie Robinson
Hali VanVliet
Monique Dowling
Matt Poepsel
Eric Koester

APPENDIX

Chapter 1: The Backward/Early Years

VIA Institute on Character. 2020. "VIA Character Strengths Survey & Character Profile Reports," Via Institute. Viacharacter.org. www.viacharacter.org.

Chapter 2: Do You Wear a Mask?

Horning, David. 2021. "Vulnerability, Risk, and Comedy at Work: How One Leader Was Able to STAND up to Traditional Leadership." *Wellness Corner* (blog), *Raleigh Metro Society for Human Resource Management.* April 23, 2021. https://rmshrm.org/david-horning-guest-blog/.

Mason, Kelli. 2022. "Study: Over 3 in 5 Are Hiding Something from Their Employer." *JobSage* (blog). April 28, 2022. https://www.jobsage.com/blog/authenticity-in-the-workplace-survey/.

"What Is Masking? 2018. *Social Psychology* (blog), *Ifioque."* Accessed February 5, 2023 www.ifioque.com. https://www.ifioque.com/social-psychology/masking.

Chapter 3: When Your Company Is Your Co-parent

Robinson, Bryan. 2021. "The Invisible Scars Adult Children of Workaholics Bring to Their Careers." *Forbes* (blog). March 8, 2021. https://www.forbes.com/sites/bryanrobinson/2021/03/08/the-invisible-scars-adult-children-of-workaholics-bring-to-their-careers.

Chapter 4: Should I Stay, or Should I Go?

Stanford Park Nannies. 2019. "The Impact of Just One Nanny." *Stanford Park Nannies* (blog). September 25, 2019. https://spnannies.com/the-impact-of-just-one-nanny.

Walker MS, Val. 2022. "Living in Limbo without Leaving People Hanging." *Psychology Today* (blog). March 29, 2022. https://www.psychologytoday.com/us/blog/400-friends-who-can-i-call/202203/living-in-limbo-without-leaving-people-hanging.

Chapter 5: Every Inch Counts When You Don't Believe You Are Enough

ADL. n.d. "Spelling of Antisemitism vs. Anti-Semitism." ADL.org. Accessed 2022. https://www.adl.org/spelling-antisemitism-vs-anti-semitism.

Brenza, Holly. 2017. "What You Need to Know about 'Leisure Sickness.'" Health Enews (blog), *AdvocateAuroraHealth*. September 25, 2017. https://www.ahchealthenews.com/2017/09/25/what-is-leisure-sickness.

Dittmann, M. 2004. "Standing Tall Pays Off, Study Finds." *Monitor on Psychology* Vol 35, No. 7, (July/August 2004): p. 14 https://www.apa.org/monitor/julaug04/standing.

Hernandez, Joe. 2021. "1 in 4 American Jews Say They Experienced Antisemitism in the Last Year." NPR, October 26, 2021. https://www.npr.org/2021/10/26/1049288223/1-in-4-american-jews-say-they-experienced-antisemitism-in-the-last-year.

Moody, Kathryn. 2022. "1 in 4 Hiring Managers Say They're Less Likely to Hire Jewish Applicants." HR Dive. November 23, 2022. https://www.hrdive.com/news/1-in-4-hiring-managers-say-theyre-less-likely-to-hire-jewish-applicants/637281/.

Chapter 6: The Business of People

Duffy, Kate. 2022. "Meta Says It's Planning to Shrink Its Office Space as More Employees Are Working Remotely." *Business Insider.* October 27, 2022. https://www.businessinsider.com/meta-office-space-employees-remote-work-from-home-zuckerberg-2022-10.

Frank, Robert. 2022. "Average Rent in Manhattan Was a Record $5,000 Last Month." CNBC. July 14, 2022. https://www.cnbc.com/2022/07/14/average-rent-in-manhattan-was-a-record-5000-last-month.html.

Fuller, David, Bryan Logan, and Aneliya Valkova. 2022. "The Great Attrition in Frontline Retail—and What Retailers Can Do about It." McKinsey & Company. Accessed September 22, 2022. https://www.mckinsey.com/industries/retail/our-insights/the-great-attrition-in-frontline-retail-and-what-retailers-can-do-about-it.

Hill, Russ. 2021. "The Great Resignation Quotes by Russ Hill." www.goodreads.com. October 19, 2021.

https://www.goodreads.com/work/quotes/93608312-the-great-resignation-why-millions-are-leaving-their-jobs-and-who-will.

National Weather Service. n.d. "What Is a Nor'easter?" Weather. gov. 2015. https://www.weather.gov/safety/winter-noreaster.

OECD. 2022. "The Unequal Impact of COVID-19: A Spotlight on Frontline Workers, Migrants and Racial/Ethnic Minorities." OECD. March 17, 2022. https://www.oecd.org/coronavirus/policy-responses/the-unequal-impact-of-covid-19-a-spotlight-on-frontline-workers-migrants-and-racial-ethnic-minorities-f36e931e/.

Renee, Navarro. 2015. "Unconscious Bias Training." UCSF. August 15, 2015. https://diversity.ucsf.edu/programs-resources/training/unconscious-bias-training.

Shevlin, Ron. 2022. "JPMorgan Chase Gets 'Work from Home' All Wrong." *Forbes* (blog). August 22, 2022. https://www.forbes.com/sites/ronshevlin/2022/08/22/jpmorgan-chase-gets-work-from-home-all-wrong/.

Tomer, Adie, and Joseph Kane. 2020. "To Protect Frontline Workers during and after COVID-19, We Must Define Who They Are." Brookings. June 10, 2020. https://www.brookings.edu/research/to-protect-frontline-workers-during-and-after-covid-19-we-must-define-who-they-are/.

Chapter 7: Take the Day Off!

Castrillon, Caroline. 2021. "Why Taking Vacation Time Could Save Your Life." *Forbes*. April 23, 2021. https://www.forbes.com/sites/carolinecastrillon/2021/05/23/why-taking-vacation-time-could-save-your-life/.

Fisher, Jen. 2015. "Workplace Burnout Survey | Deloitte US."
Deloitte United States. 2015. https://www2.deloitte.com/us/
en/pages/about-deloitte/articles/burnout-survey.html.

Gostick, Adrian, and Scott Christopher. 2023. "The Levity Effect:
Three Reasons Why It Pays for Leaders to Lighten up at Work
| Women for Hire." Women for Hire. February 5, 2023.
http://womenforhire.com/magazine/the-levity-effect-three-
reasons-why-it-pays-for-leaders-to-lighten-up-at-work/.

Gump, Brooks B., and Karen A. Matthews. 2000. "Are Vacations
Good for Your Health? The 9-Year Mortality Experience after
the Multiple Risk Factor Intervention Trial." *Psychosomatic
Medicine* 62 (5): 608-12. https://doi.org/10.1097/00006842-
200009000-00003.

"How Americans Plan to Vacation during Covid-19 - IPX1031,"
July 31, 2020. https://www.ipx1031.com/vacation-during-covid/.

Johnson MA, LPCC, Charlotte. 2022. "Stuck on Negative
Thinking." Care-Clinics.com. 2022. https://care-clinics.com/
stuck-on-negative-thinking/.

Marilisaraccoglobal. 2017. "How Taking a Vacation Can Save Your
Life – National | Globalnews.ca." Global News. June 13, 2017.
https://globalnews.ca/news/3520970/how-taking-a-vacation-
can-save-your-life.

May, Adewale. 2019. "No-Vacation Nation, Revised." Center for
Economic and Policy Research. 2019. https://cepr.net/report/
no-vacation-nation-revised/.

Nadrich, Ora. 2022. "We Have 60,000 Thoughts Each Day: Here's
How to Generate Thoughts That Matter." Addicted 2 Success.
March 6, 2022. https://addicted2success.com/life/we-have-
60000-thoughts-each-day-heres-how-to-generate-thoughts-
that-matter/.

Petrone, Paul. 2017. "How to Calculate the Cost of Employee
Disengagement." March 24, 2017. https://www.linkedin.com/

business/learning/blog/learner-engagement/how-to-calculate-the-cost-of-employee-disengagement.

Robin, Robinson. 2017. "Four Reasons to Take a Vacation." www.apadivisions.org. 2017. https://www.apadivisions.org/division-28/publications/newsletters/psychopharmacology/2017/07/vacation.

Rozentals, Artis. 2022. "Council Post: The Hustle Culture Has No Future—Enter the Break Culture." *Forbes*. April 19, 2022. https://www.forbes.com/sites/forbesbusinesscouncil/2022/04/29/the-hustle-culture-has-no-future-enter-the-break-culture/.

Sara, Clemence. 2021. "5 Reasons You Need to Take a Vacation, According to Science (Video)." Travel + Leisure. August 23, 2021. https://www.travelandleisure.com/trip-ideas/yoga-wellness/why-vacation-matters-the-science-of-taking-time-off.

"Take a Vacation for Your Heart's Sake." 2020. Be Well SHBP. March 23, 2020. https://bewellshbp.com/heart-health/take-a-vacation-for-your-hearts-sake/.

Chapter 8: The Curse of the Dreaded Fitted Sheet

Greengrass, Carla. 2021. "What Does Energy Have to Do with Leadership and Management?" *iPEC* (blog). March 17, 2021. https://www.ipeccoaching.com/blog/what-does-energy-have-to-do-with-leadership.

Noordegraaf, Simone. 2016. "What Is Core Energy Coaching?" *iPEC* (blog). July 26, 2018. https://www.ipeccoaching.com/blog/what-is-core-energy-coaching.

SHRM. 2019. "SHRM Reports Toxic Workplace Cultures Cost Billions." 2019. *SHRM* (press release). September 25, 2019. https://www.shrm.org/about-shrm/press-room/press-releases/

Pages/SHRM-Reports-Toxic-Workplace-Cultures-Cost-
Billions.aspx.

Chapter 9: Rome Wasn't Built in a Day

Betz, Eric. 2020. "If Rome Wasn't Built in a Day, How Long
Did It Take?" *Discover Magazine* (blog). November 30, 2020.
https://www.discovermagazine.com/planet-earth/if-rome-
wasnt-built-in-a-day-how-long-did-it-take.

Scuderi, Royale. 2013. "The Number One Secret to Life Success:
Baby Steps." *Lifehack* (blog). January 25, 2013.
https://www.lifehack.org/articles/communication/secret-to-
life-success-baby-steps.html.

Chapter 10: I Am a Recovering Workaholic

Brummelhuis, Lieke ten, and Nancy P. Rothbard. 2018. "How
Being a Workaholic Differs from Working Long Hours—and
Why That Matters for Your Health." *Harvard Business Review*
(blog). March 22, 2018. https://hbr.org/2018/03/how-being-a-
workaholic-differs-from-working-long-hours-and-why-that-
matters-for-your-health.

Robinson, Bryan. 2021. "The Invisible Scars Adult Children of
Workaholics Bring to Their Careers." *Forbes* (blog). March 8,
2021. https://www.forbes.com/sites/bryanrobinson/2021/03/08/
the-invisible-scars-adult-children-of-workaholics-bring-to-
their-careers/.

Schmall, Tyler. 2019. "Almost Half of Americans Consider Themselves 'Workaholics.'" *New York Post*. February 1, 2019.

https://nypost.com/2019/02/01/almost-half-of-americans-consider-themselves-workaholics/.

Chapter 11: Thirty-Three and Me

Ahmed, Shah Alif. 2022. "Workplace Spirituality: What It Is and How to Foster It." *Company Culture* (blog), *Vantage Circle*. August 10, 2022. https://blog.vantagecircle.com/workplace-spirituality/.

Aletheia. 2022. "Synchronicity and the Meaning of Numbers." *LonerWolf*. December 6, 2022. https://lonerwolf.com/meaning-of-numbers/.

Garrett, R. Kelly. 2017. "Should We Worry That Half of Americans Trust Their Gut to Tell Them What's True?" *The Conversation*. September 27, 2017. https://theconversation.com/should-we-worry-that-half-of-americans-trust-their-gut-to-tell-them-whats-true-84259.

Lui, Ana. 2016. "33 Is the Magic Number for Being 33 Forever." *Ana Lui Photography* (blog). May 7, 2016. https://www.analuiphotography.com/blog/33-is-the-magic-number.

Weitzner, David. 2022. "What Is Spirituality at Work?" *Psychology Today* (blog). March 18, 2022. https://www.psychologytoday.com/us/blog/managing-with-meaning/202203/what-is-spirituality-at-work.

Chapter 12: The Grievance of Grief

Huget, Jennifer. 2003. "Orphaned at Middle Age." *Washington Post*, November 25, 2003. https://www.washingtonpost.com/

archive/lifestyle/wellness/2003/11/25/orphaned-at-middle-age/
7f616a06-0b0c-418c-8c64-2905da707665/.

Mallick, Mita. 2020. "It's Time to Rethink Corporate Bereavement Policies." *Harvard Business Review* (blog). October 5,
2020. https://hbr.org/2020/10/its-time-to-rethink-corporate-
bereavement-policies.

Thompson, Rachel. 2017. "Facebook's New Bereavement Leave
Raises an Important Point about Grief in the Workplace."
Mashable. February 10, 2017. https://mashable.com/article/
facebook-grief-policy.

Chapter 13: No One Does It Alone

Fisher, Anne. 2007. "Being a Mentor Could Boost Your Own
Career – Mar. 13, 2007." Money.cnn.com. March 13, 2007.
https://money.cnn.com/2007/03/12/news/economy/mentoring.
fortune/index.htm.

Weidinger, Steve. 2020. "What Are the Benefits of Having a
Workplace Mentor?" Washington Post Jobs. July 20, 2020.
https://jobs.washingtonpost.com/article/what-are-the-benefits-
of-having-a-workplace-mentor-/.

"Why Mentoring: What the Stats Say." 2017. McCarthy Mentoring |
Inspiring Leaders. May 22, 2017. https://mccarthymentoring.com/
why-mentoring-what-the-stats-say/.

Chapter 14: The Cost of Change

Brown, Brené. 2015a. *Rising Strong.* New York: Spiegel & Grau
(Random House).

Williams, Rachelle. 2019. "The Power of Giving and Receiving: Which One Is Better?" Chopra. December 2, 2019. https://chopra.com/articles/the-power-of-giving-and-receiving-which-one-is-better.

Printed in Great Britain
by Amazon

26850346R00109